If you were

arrested

for being kind

to yourself . . .

. . . would there

be enough

evidence

to convict you?

PRELUDE:
What If?

What if you were about to meet your perfect lover?

What if you knew this lover better than anyone else in the world, and this lover knew you better than anyone else?

What if you liked the same food, loved the same movies, listened to the same music, rooted for the same teams, enjoyed the same friends, were fascinated by the same books, had the same spiritual beliefs, cared about the same causes, and shared the same goals?

What if you absolutely knew you two could live together comfortably?

What if this lover always had your best interests at heart?

What if you were brought before a large door and told that, behind the door, was the love of your life?

You straighten your hair, pop a Certs, take a deep breath, open the door . . .

. . . and find yourself face-to-face . . .

. . . with a mirror.

INTERVIEWER:

How do you do?

MAE WEST:

How do you do <u>what</u>?

Author's Notes

In the early 1970s, I went to the American Book-sellers Association annual convention, where publishers rent booths at exorbitant rates and show their recent wares to the booksellers of America. At the Penguin booth, I saw a book entitled *Self Love*. It had an introduction by Alan Watts, who was then and is still my favorite philosopher. I was excited to discover a book about the love of oneself endorsed by him and published by such a distinguished house as Penguin—then known primarily for its reprints of the classics. As was the custom at ABA, complimentary copies were available. I took my copy and thanked the salesperson, a dignified British man who nodded his acceptance of my appreciation.

"I can really use this book," I said. "I'm very bad at self-love."

The sales representative smiled one of those smiles that doesn't go up at the edges, but merely makes one's mouth wider while perfectly horizontal.

"In fact, of all the things I need to work on," I continued, "I think self-love is the most essential." I was twenty-something at the time, and determined to be "open about my process." I could see, however, that saying I didn't know how to love myself made the Penguin sales representative a bit uncomfortable, so I said my good-bye.

"Thank you again," I said, extending my hand. As he shook it, I said, "In fact, I'm going up to my hotel room right now and read this." He dropped my hand.

> *The last time I saw him*
> *he was walking down Lover's Lane*
> *holding his own hand.*
>
> FRED ALLEN

The Penguin book on self-love was about the joys of masturbation.

My seeking self-love in the early 1970s was sincere. Like many people, I had inhaled the book *How to Be Your Own Best Friend*. I read it clandestinely—it seemed to be as taboo a subject as that *other* form of self-love. In 1971, the idea that one could be one's own friend, much less *best* friend, was radical.

Today, the notion that one can be the most significant love object in one's own life, is just as radical.

I certainly do not present myself as a pillar of self-loving, nor put myself on a pedestal labeled AN

IDEAL SPECIMEN OF A SELF-LOVING PERSON. I'm just a person who has been struggling with the notion of loving himself since 1967. Twenty-eight years later, I finally feel as though I have *something* worth sharing; that I know enough about the subject to write a book on it; and, since there's something more to learn about everything, "The best way to learn about a subject," Benjamin Disraeli once said, "is to write a book about it."

Although your path and discoveries on the road to greater self-love will differ from mine, allow me to offer three personal observations:

1. God* is within you.**

2. You are lovable, *just as you are now.*

3. You *can* learn to love yourself, more and more each day.

In this book I will not be spending a great deal of time on point #1. The discovery of, defining of, relating to, and praise for God I will leave to you, God, and any number of excellent source materials on the subject. *LOVE 101* can be read by anyone, from devout fundamentalist to confirmed atheist, and he or she can learn enough about self-loving to proclaim, "Glory, hallelujah! I'm glad I read this book."

---

*As you perceive him, her, or it to be, from God the Father, to Mother Nature, to Universal Mind, to the "illimitable superior spirit who reveals himself in the slight details we are able to perceive with our frail and feeble mind" (Einstein).

**For those who find this an anti-Christian statement, please consider this from Jesus: "The kingdom of God is within you" (Luke 17:21).

> *Style is knowing who you are,*
> *what you want to say,*
> *and not giving a damn.*
>
> GORE VIDAL

In the end, of course, we must all write our own book on how to love ourselves. Thanks for reading my book. My best and warmest wishes to you as you write your own.

Take good care,

Peter McWilliams
Los Angeles, California
January 3, 1995

P.S. LOVE 101: *To Love Oneself Is the Beginning of a Lifelong Romance* was completed on January 3, 1995. Precisely one hundred years earlier—to the day—the curtain rose at London's Theatre Royal on Oscar Wilde's latest play, *An Ideal Husband*. As the third act opens, we find this stage direction:

Enter LORD GORING *in evening dress with a button hole [flower in his lapel]. He is wearing a silk hat and Inverness cape. White-gloved, he carries a Louis Seize cane. His are all the delicate fopperies of fashion. One sees that he stands in immediate relation to modern life, makes it, indeed, and so masters it. He is the first well-dressed philosopher in the history of thought.*

Could Wilde possibly be describing himself? But of course. Goring addresses his butler:

LORD GORING: You see, Phipps, fashion is what one wears oneself. Whereas un-fashionable is what other people wear.

PHIPPS: Yes, my lord.

LORD GORING: Just as vulgarity is simply the conduct of other people.

PHIPPS: Yes, my lord.

LORD GORING [putting in new button hole]: And falsehoods the truths of other people.

PHIPPS: Yes, my lord.

LORD GORING: To love oneself is the beginning of a lifelong romance.

PHIPPS: Yes, my lord.

And from that bit of typical Wilde dialogue comes the subtitle for this book.

*To fall in love
with yourself
is the first secret
of happiness.*

*I did so at the age
of four-and-a-half.*

*Then if you're not
a good mixer
you can always
fall back on
your own company.*

ROBERT MORLEY

INTRODUCTION:
You Are Already Living
with the Love of Your Life

This is a book about a myth and a taboo.

THE MYTH: In order to be complete and ful-filled, you must find one "significant other" to love. This significant other must consider you his or her significant other and love you back with equal devo-tion till death do you part.

THE TABOO: It is somehow unwholesome to love yourself.

In *LOVE 101* I'll be challenging both the myth and the taboo. If you're not ready to have these challenged, it would be best if you stop reading now—this book will only upset you.

If, on the other hand, you have been gradually coming to the seemingly forbidden conclusion that before we can truly love another, or allow another to properly love us, we must first learn to love our-selves—then this book is for you.

The taboo that we shouldn't love ourselves is one of the silliest in modern culture. Who else is more qualified to love you than you? Who else knows what you want, precisely when you want it, and is always around to supply it?

Who do you go to bed with, sleep with, dream with, shower with, eat with, work with, play with, pray with, go to the movies with, and watch TV with?

> *The continued propinquity*
> *of another human being*
> *cramps your style after a time*
> *unless that person*
> *is somebody you think you love.*
>
> *Then the burden*
> *becomes intolerable at once.*
>
> QUENTIN CRISP

Who else knows where it itches, and just how hard to scratch it?

Who are you reading this book with?

Who have you always lived with, and whom will you eventually die with?

And, who will be the only person to accompany you on that ultimate adventure (just think of death as a theme park with a high admission cost), while all your *other* loved ones are consoling each other by saying how happy you must be with God and how natural you look?

Spiritually, who is the only person who can join you in your relationship with God, Jesus, Buddha, Mohammed, Moses, Mother Nature, The Force, Creative Intelligence, or whomever or whatever you consider to be the moving force of existence?

And, who has been there every time you've had sex?*

So, from the sacred to the profane (and all points in between), your ideal lover is *you*.

Then why is loving ourselves such a taboo? Why is the notion that we *need* another to love (who will love us back) such an enormous myth?

In a word, control.

The self-contained, emotionally autonomous, intellectually free individual is the greatest threat to the institutions that want to control us. Those of us who refuse to act like sheep—who question authority and want genuine answers, not just knee-jerk clichés—are a pain in the *gluteus maximus* (and regions nearby) to those who want to rule by *power* rather than by providing *leadership*.

We see attempts to manipulate almost everywhere—in politics, religion, advertising, entertainment.

When we are programmed to "fall" for the hunk or the honey of a certain aesthetic type, and to believe that these images of sex and beauty mean "true love," then these images can be used to sell us anything from cigarettes to movie tickets. And they are, they are.

---

*Yes, from time to time others may have been nearby doing what they could to help, but whatever pleasure you felt was inside yourself, experienced in those inner electrochemical, physiological pleasure places that are entirely your own. This is true for *anything* pleasurable we see, feel, hear, touch, or taste: without *our senses* nothing "out there"—from movies to pepperoni pizza—would be in the least enjoyable.

> *Conformity
> is the jailer of freedom
> and the enemy of growth.*
>
> JOHN F. KENNEDY

Further, when the only "moral" outcome of a romantic relationship is a till-death-do-us-part, state-licensed, church-blessed marriage, we see the fundamental forces of conformity at work. If we're all the *same*, we are much easier to *serve*—also sell to, also control.

If we're all the same—and marriage is one of the best homogenizers around—then we only need one religion, one political party: the Family Values Party. In fact, why not combine religion and government in one?

That's been the history of the world—church and state hand-in-hand, slavish conformity, and those troublemakers (ungodly and unpatriotic) who fail to shape up . . . well, there have always been ways of dealing with *them*.

But this book is not a political diatribe. It's a book about personal freedom—the freedom to choose the life you want, even though the powers that be think you should not do so. They know best.

Except they don't. More than half the people in this country live outside the "traditional" mama-papa-children household. It hasn't worked.

Please understand that I am not against family, marriage, children, or even romance. I am merely against the idea that we should *all* be herded into that mode of relating when there are viable, satisfying alternatives (which we'll explore later in this book).

There will always be people who want to get married and raise children. More power to them. The trouble arises when people who want to do something *else* (write, pray, save the dolphins) get married and have children because they think they *should*, not because they *want to*.

This clutters up the marriage market with un-qualified players—those who would rather be training for a decathlon just don't have the same *commitment* to child-rearing. So, they drop out of the marriage—emotionally or entirely—and the other partner, who still *wants* a marriage, wonders, "What happened?"

What happened is what happens every time we are all programmed to do the same thing—those who don't really want to be there muck it up for those who do.

If a group of people were all taken to an opera one night, a rock concert the second night, the latest Woody Allen movie the third night, and an

> *Mass democracy, mass morality*
> *and the mass media thrive*
> *independently of the individual,*
> *who joins them only at the cost*
> *of at least a partial perversion*
> *of his instinct and insights.*
>
> *He pays for his social ease*
> *with what used to be called his soul,*
> *his discriminations, his uniqueness,*
> *his psychic energy, his self.*
>
> AL ALVAREZ

Englebert Humperdink concert the fourth, chances are that on at least one of those nights, some of the audience would be, to paraphrase S. J. Pearlman, if not disgruntled, certainly not fully gruntled.

If, on the other hand, each individual in the group had a choice to go to any, all, or none of the four, then self-selection would lead to far more gruntled audiences at *all* the events.

This book is about you getting more gruntled in *all* your relationships—especially your relationship with yourself.

You'll note I've only talked about the failure of marriage. Imagine how much more unsuccessful romance is. There are two million divorces in the United States each year. Is it fair to estimate that for every divorce there are at least ten break-ups between nonmarried romantics? If so, there are, counting the newly divorced, twenty-two million broken hearts littering the emotional landscape. There are also twenty-two million (the ones who did the dumping) who are proclaiming "Free at last!"

And yet the majority of those millions, who now have already had first-hand experience that a romantic relationship doesn't necessarily lead to a lifelong happy marriage, will *again* be jumping into the next acceptable pair of eyes, or thighs, that come along. "The *person* was the problem," they tell themselves. "If only I find the right *person*." Maybe it's the *type of relationship* that's not working. Maybe.

What does it cost *us* to fall for this myth that we *must* find another to love, and *must* (in the same person) find someone to love us? It costs us the loving, laughing, emotionally stable, intellectually stimulating, and physically satisfying relationship with the person perfectly qualified to be our best friend in this lifetime—*ourselves*.

We trade the ongoing, here-and-now, potentially vibrant, fun-filled, nurturing relationship with ourselves for some future promise of Prince Charming or Cinderella riding in on a white charger or a refurbished pumpkin, transforming our lives with True Love. That's like not eating your home-cooked food because you have been convinced that any day now (real soon), a gourmet (not just *any* gourmet, mind you, but your own personal star-crossed gourmet) will appear—pots, pans, leeks, and all.

Am I saying you should turn the gourmet away? *Not at all.* Being with others, sharing with others,

> *Love, love, love—all the wretched cant of it, masking egotism, lust, masochism, fantasy under a mythology of sentimental postures, a welter of self induced miseries and joys, blinding and masking the essential personalities in the frozen gestures of courtship, in the kissing and the dating and the desire, the compliments and the quarrels which vivify its barrenness.*
>
> GERMAINE GREER

supporting and being supported by others are among the most fulfilling activities we can enjoy. I'm simply saying that loving oneself *while* loving others makes *all* interactions more enjoyable.

Some even say that loving oneself is a *prerequisite* to loving others. I won't take it quite that far, but I do know loving oneself is an *important* part of loving others (and allowing others to love you).

When we are already loving and loved by ourselves, our desire to love and be loved by others is just that—a desire. We no longer have the burning, aching *need* to love and be loved. Back in my desperately seeking-another-to-love-who-will-love-me-back days, I wrote a poem:

My needs destroy
the paths
through which
those needs
could be
fulfilled.

I had on my wall in letters a foot tall, the needy
proclamation taken from Peter Townsend's *Tommy:*

SEE ME

FEEL ME

TOUCH ME

HEAL ME

Talk about an *intimidating* message to present to
the newly met.

At seventeen, my muse gave me the answer. I
was sitting in a coffee shop as the sun was coming
up and wrote on a paper napkin (as all poets do
from time to time):

I must conquer my loneliness
alone.

I must be happy with myself
or I have
nothing
to offer.

Two halves have
little choice
but to
join,
and yes,
they do

> *I am two fools, I know,*
> *For loving, and for saying so*
> *In whining poetry*
>
> JOHN DONNE
> 1572–1631

make a
whole.

But two
wholes,
when they coincide . . .

that is
beauty.

That is
love.

It took me some time—with any number of false starts, dead ends, and dashed hopes*—to get the wisdom of this edict off the napkin and into my life.

*But I did sell a large pile of poetry books along the way! When life gives you lemons, write *The Lemon Cookbook.*

LOVE 101 is what I learned along the way. You may have a different way with different learnings, but I pray that some of my musings you'll find useful, inspiring, or amusing.

I wrote this book for myself—a collection of what I have learned about self-loving so that if I fall into a pit of self-loathing (an inevitability—what lovers don't have quarrels?), I will have these reminders to help me de-pit myself.

I hope you'll read along in my "manual on loving me" and make as much of it your own as you care to.

*There is only
one success—
to spend your life
in your own way.*

CHRISTOPHER MORLEY

LOVE 101

*To Love Oneself
Is the Beginning
of a Lifelong Romance*

Peter McWilliams

Prelude Press
8159 Santa Monica Boulevard
Los Angeles, California 90046

1-800-LIFE-101

This book is available on unabridged audiocassette tapes,
read by the author.

The quotes in this book are taken from
a number of sources, the best of which is
Jon Winokur's collection, *A Curmudgeon's Garden of Love*.

The front and back covers are by Maxfield Parrish.
The back cover is *Stars* (1926), and the front cover
is *Harvest*, painted (unbelievably) in 1905.
Design by Peter McWilliams and Victoria Marine

ISBN: 0-931580-72-2

Editors: Jean Sedillos and Victoria Marine
Desktop publisher: Victoria Marine
Production assistant: Mary Jane Deal
Editorial assistants: Wendy Cohen, Zac Cook,
Bruce Eaton, Barbara Hutnick, Linda Krasnoff

*I've married
a few people
I shouldn't have,
but haven't
we all?*

MAMIE VAN DOREN

Other Books by Peter McWilliams

DO IT! Let's Get Off Our Buts

LIFE 101: Everything We Wish We Had Learned About Life In School—But Didn't

LIFE 102: What to Do When Your Guru Sues You

You Can't Afford the Luxury of a Negative Thought: A Book for People with Any Life-Threatening Illness—Including Life

Focus on the Positive: The You Can't Afford the Luxury of a Negative Thought Workbook

WEALTH 101: Wealth Is Much More Than Money

We Give to Love: Giving Is Such a Selfish Thing

How to Heal Depression (with Harold H. Bloomfield, M.D.)

How to Survive the Loss of a Love (with Melba Colgrove, Ph.D., and Harold H. Bloomfield, M.D.)

Surviving, Healing and Growing: The How to Survive the Loss of a Love Workbook (with Melba Colgrove, Ph.D., and Harold H. Bloomfield, M.D.)

Come Love With Me & Be My Life: The Complete Romantic Poetry of Peter McWilliams (Sorry!)

I Marry You Because . . .

PORTRAITS: A Book of Photographs

Ain't Nobody's Business If You Do: The Absurdity of Consensual Crimes in a Free Society

That Book About Drugs

What Jesus and the Bible Really Said About Drugs, Sex, Gays, Gambling, Prostitution, Alternative Healing, Assisted Suicide, and Other Consensual "Sins"

*Freedom is not
something that
anybody
can be given.*

*Freedom is
something
people take,
and people
are as free
as they
want to be.*

JAMES BALDWIN

Dedication

I would like to dedicate this book,
with love,
to Peter McWilliams,
who has stuck with me
through thick and thin,
lean times and lush times,
and without whom
this book would have been
improbable.

*We define genius
as the capacity for
productive reaction
against one's training.*

<small>BERNARD BERENSON</small>

Contents

If there were
in the world today
any large number
of people
who desired
their own happiness
more than
they desired
the unhappiness of others,
we could have a paradise
in a few years.

BERTRAND RUSSELL

LOVE 101

To Love Oneself
Is the Beginning
of a Lifelong Romance

*If love is
the answer,
could you
rephrase
the question?*

LILY TOMLIN

Self-Love vs. Romantic Love

When I talk about loving yourself, what sort of love do I mean? Simply this:

Love is taking care of,
with regular intervals of taking good care of,
and occasional splurges of pampering.

In this book, I am merely suggesting that you take care of yourself, regularly take *good* care of yourself, and every so often indulge yourself in a little pampering.

This is quite a different definition of love than the one offered by the proponents of "falling in love." Their love is an emotional bungee-jump from the depths to the heights of romance. Being "in love" generally implies people have "lost themselves" in someone (or at least the *illusion* of what that other person comprises), are obsessed by the other person (and relishing the addiction), and are desperate for the other person to feel the same way about them.

This form of love I shall refer to as *romantic love*. Essential to romantic love but (thankfully) missing from self-love, is an overwhelming, all consuming *lust*. What sort of lust? What sort have you got?

Sexual lust? Oh, my, yes. Although it is hidden behind any number of high-sounding platitudes, the need to do the dirty deed—and do it *magnificently* (and often)—is central to those "in love." The need for intense physical union, each to each, that obliterates physical boundaries and hurls one to the heavens, is a high-sounding way of saying, "I've got the hots for you."

> *Love ain't nothing*
> *but sex misspelled.*
>
> HARLAN ELLISON

Someday we are going to be lovers.
Maybe married.
At the least, an affair.
What's your name?

Then there is emotional lust. We want the loved one to be *ours*, just as we want to be fully possessed by the one we love. This emotional bonding should be so tight that not only is there no room for emotional need; there is no *thought* of emotional need. All needs are met, once and for all, in the mutual clutching, that is, *embrace* of the lovers.

The term "spiritual lust" may seem to be an oxymoron, but not in the world of romantic love. Here lovers meet, soul to soul, "and this union is a reunion with creation" (as the romantic poet in me once put it). Nothing less than *God* is to be found in the physical, emotional, mental, and spiritual fusion of star-crossed lovers. Being in love is not just finding a mate; it is finding a *soul* mate. That spiritual "other half" (or "better half") that we have been deprived of since before birth has finally, at last, thank God, been given unto us and we can finally, at last, thank God, get on with the business of temporal bliss on earth and rehearse for the eternal bliss hereafter.

The belief that the beloved is God-given also goes a long way to remove any *guilt* interfering with the free, unfettered, and fabulous expression of the other lusts—especially sex.

Ordinary, everyday self-love, by comparison, is gentler, easier on the physiology. What it lacks in passion, it makes up for in practicality. Where it falls short in lust, it makes up for in like. What it fails to provide in false security ("I'll take care of you until the end of time!"), it makes up for in self-esteem, self-worth, and self-reliance. What it lacks in sexual yah-yahs, it makes up for in sensual umm-umms.

In learning to love ourselves in this "taking care of" way, we also learn to love others—to take care of them, to occasionally take *good* care of them, and every so often (when we choose) to indulge them shamelessly.

Loving others, then, becomes part of loving ourselves if, when, and as we choose.

Not that romance can't be fun. It can. So can a roller coaster.

It's when we confuse the ride with real life or

> *Hard work is damn near*
> *as overrated as monogamy.*
>
> HUEY P. LONG

use it to make choices that have nothing to do with roller coasters that we get into trouble. As Stephen Sondheim put it, "the net descends."

Let's say we *love* the roller coaster and all the endorphins and adrenalin it produces. That doesn't mean that we should ever consider *living* on the roller coaster, or try to combine a roller-coaster life with career seeking, tranquility, or child rearing.

No, roller coaster rides are roller coaster rides and are compatible with loud music, screaming, losing your lunch (or at least the near occasion of losing your lunch), wind-blown hair, and not much else. If you desire and pursue the roller coaster above all else, then all else (especially those activities requiring tranquility, reflection, stability, nurturing, and quiet enjoyment) will not prevail.

Unless you want to run off with the carnival, letting a roller coaster (or, worse, Tunnel of Love) ride determine the rest of your life is, obviously, impractical.

And yet, that's just what we try to do with romantic love and the rest of our lives.

Romantic love
is mental illness.
But it's a pleasurable one.
It's a drug.
It distorts reality,
and that's the point of it.
It would be impossible
to fall in love
with someone
that you really <u>saw</u>.

FRAN LEBOWITZ

The Myth of Romantic Love: Living off the Fat of Infatuation

Romantic love is, quite literally, a drug high. The intensely good feeling of "falling in love" is triggered by the same physiological reactions caused by free-fall in sky diving or winning a fortune in the lottery. Free-fall, fortune winning, and falling in love release into the bloodstream epinephrine, commonly known as adrenaline (the body's natural *hey-hey-hey!* chemical) and endorphins (the body's *whoopee!* chemical). These chemicals are just as pleasurable as any drugs (licit or illicit) you care to name—and just as addictive.

It's an addiction, however, our society not only tolerates, but *encourages.* According to cultural norms, addiction to heroin, cocaine, or alcohol is bad. Addiction to the thrill of falling in love is good. In fact, *not* being addicted to love is bad. Further, being "in love" is reason enough to do almost anything—from murder to abandoning one's career.

It is hard to name anything that gets more free positive publicity than romantic love. Every movie, commercial, TV show (sitcom, drama, or movie-of-the-week), popular song, billboard, and nine out of ten bestsellers sing the praises of romantic love.

It is painful to watch how tortured the plots become in order to work in the "love interest," as it's known in Hollywood. How is it that Indiana Jones

> *Human beings seem to have*
> *an almost unlimited capacity*
> *to deceive themselves and*
> *to deceive themselves*
> *into taking*
> *their own lies*
> *for the truth.*
>
> *One's only task is to realize oneself.*
>
> R. D. LAING

always seems to find at least one gorgeous, intelligent, but otherwise romantically available woman in the midst of the jungle, desert, Incan ruins, Egyptian pyramids, or Peking opium den? Why? Well, as George Lucas once advised Steven Spielberg, "If the man and woman walk off into the sunset hand-in-hand in the last reel, it adds $10 million to the box office."

Romantic love is used so often because it sells so well, and the media always have something to sell. As they are using romantic love to sell what they want to sell (higher ratings, soap, Fenamint, books, tickets), they are also selling the notion of romantic love itself. This means romance sells better, which means it's used more often to sell, so it gets sold even more often, and so on. It's a very successful marketing tool.

From the consumer's point of view, however, there is only one small problem with romantic love: it's almost always doomed to failure.

*The consuming desire
of most human beings
is deliberately to plant
their whole life
in the hands
of some other person.*

*For this purpose
they frequently choose someone
who doesn't even want
the beastly thing.*

*I would describe this method
of searching for happiness
as immature.*

*Development of character
consists solely
in moving towards
self-sufficiency.*

QUENTIN CRISP

Why Romantic Love Is Almost Always Doomed

Few enterprises fail as often and as traumatically as romantic love, yet are still considered by many not just *a* solution, but *the* solution.

Solution to what? You name it: love waltzes in and dances your problems away. From solving the fundamental "problem" of existence to renewed health to financial rejuvenation to a cure for loneliness, Prince Charming or Cinderella cureth all.

At the outset, perhaps this is true. The problem, however, with this all-purpose problem solver is that it is based almost entirely on *illusion*.

We are programmed with the illusion of romantic love from an early age. The same culture that programs us to believe in Santa Claus, the Easter Bunny, the Tooth Fairy, and Free Lunch also programs us to believe in One Significant Other Out There Without Whom We Can't Be Whole, Much Less Happy. Minnie and Mickey, Olive Oyl and Popeye, Barbie and Ken, Lady and the Tramp—and they all lived happily ever after.

Right.

Mercifully, by the time we reach puberty and the advent of all those raging hormones that form the biochemical basis of romantic love, we have been disillusioned (probably traumatically) about Santa Claus, the Easter Bunny, the Tooth Fairy, and (for some) Free Lunch. Alas, as the early teenage years progress and our throbbing hormones create

> *In real love*
> *you want the other person's good.*
>
> *In romantic love*
> *you want the other person.*
>
> Margaret Anderson

desires for other people's bodies which easily surpass even the most meaningful childhood visitation to Toys R Us, the illusion of romantic love is not dispelled. In fact, the spell is cast deeper, stronger, in Technicolor, 3-D, Dolby ProLogic, Sensearound-sound, and feelaroundbound.

We are taught (by songs, movies, TV shows) that the natural physical attractions of the early teenage years are all part of the romantic ideal. It is "the dawn of love," "love at first sight," or "if you call it horny your parents will ground you, but if you say you're in love your parents will say it's a crush and whisper 'Oh, how cute!'"

We are told the attraction—which is biochemical and electrical, but feels downright *magnetic*—is just the *start* of Something Big. "You mean it gets better than *this?*" Oh, yes, the more deeply you fall in love, the more spectacular it becomes. "Love Is a Many Splendored Thing."

To quote another song (you can discourse on romantic love's philosophy by quoting almost *any* song), "Fools Rush in Where Wise Men Fear to Tread." If this is true (and it probably is, if you consider that even the wise can become foolish when hormones and cultural programming combine to lower the IQ roughly one hundred points, as it does when one is about to fall in love), the wise are distressingly silent when it comes to teaching us about a certain biological imperative common to all mammals.

Rather than saying, for example, "Yes, this is a perfectly natural, healthy reaction, but it is not practical to act on it every time you feel it any more than it is practical to eat every morsel of food you see. Sexual attraction is just energy; if the time is not right to express it sexually, for whatever reason, then the energy can be used to create something else that is productive, satisfying, and fun."

No, the wise seem to have had their wisdom co-opted by the Grand Illusion. Some of the wise tales sound more like old wives' tales. "This feeling you have will deepen into desire, ripen into passion, grow into fulfillment, and flower into love." That even the wise want to escape the birds and the bees and instead discuss *flowers* is indicative of just how far from reality those who sell us the notion of romantic love must go.

> The message that "love" will solve
> all of our problems is repeated incessantly
> in contemporary culture—
> like a philosophical tom tom.
>
> It would be closer to the truth to say
> that love is a contagious and virulent
> disease which leaves a victim
> in a state of near imbecility,
> paralysis, profound melancholia,
> and sometimes culminates in death.
>
> QUENTIN CRISP

As *animals*, we have more in common with birds and bees than we do with flowers. Most birds pair up for a season. They build a nest, mate, lay eggs, sit on eggs, feed the young for a few weeks, kick the kids out of the nest, and fly south for a well-deserved winter vacation—alone. In the spring, they fly north and begin it all again, usually with a new partner. With the exception of a few species including some lesbian sea gulls off the coast of California, to birds "till death do us part" means that they are living amongst a larger-than-usual population of pussy cats.

And of bees, well, allow Phyllis Lindstrom, of *The Mary Tyler Moore Show* to explain:

> Did you know the male bee is nothing but the slave of the queen? And once the male bee has, how should I say, *serviced* the queen, the male dies. All in all, not a bad system.

By the time we've reached dating age, the emotionally seductive concepts of "someone to watch over me," "in the morning, in the evening, ain't we got fun?" and "they all lived happily ever after" form an almost irresistible package, which has us by the end of the fifteen-year romance infomercial picking up our phones, dialing the number, and proclaiming, "I want it! I want it! I want it *now!*"

As with most illusions, reality inevitably intervenes, causing hurt, anger, and the exceptional success of broken-hearted love ballads. Unlike other disappointments, however, reality intervening in romantic love fails to bring disillusion. We still believe in romantic love; we just think *we* didn't measure up or *they* didn't measure up. Next time, we believe—next person, next weekend, next year, next lifetime it will be better, it will happen—true love, *true love.* To believe that the illusion is real, but that the loved one or our ability to love is inadequate, is of course all part of the illusion.

I'm not saying romantic love can't lead to solid, healthy, flexible, mutually nourishing relationships—sometimes it does, and sometimes it doesn't. But it's not a sure thing. Fifty-four percent of the marriages in this country end in divorce, and that's

> *When two people are*
> *under the influence of the most violent,*
> *most insane, most delusive,*
> *and most transient of passions,*
> *they are required to swear*
> *that they will remain in that excited,*
> *abnormal, and exhausting condition*
> *continuously*
> *until death do them part.*
>
> GEORGE BERNARD SHAW

just the *marriages*. As we explored, if we add to that the number of people who fall in love "forever and ever" and break up before getting married, it's clear that what we are doing to achieve "happily ever after" ain't working.

Jack Parr, who was raised vegetarian, said that, as a child, every time he passed a butcher's window he thought there had been a terrible accident. It is not hard to come to the same conclusion as one surveys the landscape of romantic love, littered as it always seems to be with wounded, broken, and bleeding hearts.

Those who say the solution is to return to "traditional family values," have obviously spent very little time studying tradition, family, or history. In fact, "the good old days" (whenever you want to peg the good old days to be) were terrible for almost everyone. To return to "the good old days" would require women to be treated as chattel; a significantly shortened lifespan; six-day, fourteen-hour-a-day work weeks; fifty percent of all children dying before the age of eight; increased disease, pestilence, suffering, and no VCRs.

Since we can't go back to an idyllic past that never existed in the first place, what *can* we do? We do what we usually do when we discover what we believed in, hoped for, longed for, and fully expected to happen (someday) is simply not true; a myth. Poof. We become the sadder, but wiser, rabbit. This prevents us from becoming the miserable and stupid rabbit who keeps banking on a payoff that is a long shot at best.

The fundamental problem with romantic love is that it is based on sexual attraction, which is, at its most reliable, fickle. Once desire dries up—in a week, a month, or a year—it's *hasta la vista*, baby. More scientifically stated, when the physical and aesthetic characteristics of the love object no longer trigger spontaneous emissions of pleasurable chemicals into the bloodstream, the amount of time spent with, and attention paid to, the former object of desire decreases in direct ratio to the decrease of pleasurable hormonal secretions. Put most simply—when lust hits the dust, it's a bust.

"Oh, but I didn't love him for his *body*," some protest at my seemingly narrow analysis. "I loved him for his *mind* (character, ideals, kindness)." That may be so, dear heart, but you can bet the reason

> *Personally, I like sex*
> *and I don't care*
> *what a man thinks of me*
> *as long as I get*
> *what I want from him—*
> *which is usually sex.*
>
> VALERIE PERRINE

your partner—the mindful, idealistic, kindly character—showed you his remarkable mind, character,
ideals, and kindness is, most likely, that he found
your body not too shabby.*

---

*The stereotype is, of course, that the man has lust in his heart
and the woman succumbs to higher qualities—such as his bill-
fold. Personally, I subscribe to very few "differences in the sexes"
theories. I have seen women fall for men who are the intellectual
equal of a weather balloon, but (to quote Sondheim again), "Oh,
could that boy fox trot!" Similarly, I have talked to any number
of men who felt "abused" and "misled" when they discovered
that their former lovers' affections were merely affectations, and
that the woman's primary attraction (now significantly diminished) was "merely physical." What I am talking about in this
book are *behaviors* (both uplifting and otherwise) in which *anyone*
can take part—whether male or female, gay or straight, bi or sell.

When two people have a mutual nonsexual attraction, seldom, if ever, do they refer to it as "falling in love" or to their being together as a "relationship." It's called a friendship, partnership, or acquaintanceship. Although the two may *grow* to love one another, they do not *fall* into anything (unless there is money or some other lust-inducing enticement) and they don't go blindly leaping off emotional cliffs, yelling, "Saint Valentine protect me! Here I go

    o

      o

        o

      o

    o

      oh-oh . . ."

       SPLAT.

From time to time great minds have risked censure, public ridicule, and the loss of research grants to speak the truth about romantic love. Here are the best I could find. (O, to have had this list when I was seventeen!)

> A mighty pain to love it is,
> And 'tis a pain that pain to miss;
> But of all pains, the greatest pain
> It is to love, but love in vain.
> —*Abraham Cowley (1656)*

> Time, which strengthens friendship, weakens love.
> —*Jean de La Bruyère (1688)*

> *My silks and fine array,*
> *My smiles and languished air,*
> *By love are driv'n away;*
> *And mournful lean Despair*
> *Brings me yew to deck my grave:*
> *Such end true lovers have.*

WILLIAM BLAKE

Beauty soon grows familiar to the lover,
Fades in his eye, and palls upon the sense.
—*Joseph Addison (1713)*

If love is judged by most of its effects, it resembles hate more than friendship.—*La Rochefoucauld*

Love is ridiculous passion which hath no being but in play-books and romances.—*Jonathan Swift*

It is impossible to love and to be wise.
—*Francis Bacon*

Love is the child of illusion and the parent of disillusion.—*Miguel de Unamuno*

Love is a springtime plant that perfumes everything with its hope, even the ruins to which it clings.—*Flaubert*

Love is a disease which fills you with a desire to be desired.—*Toulouse-Lautrec*

Never the time and the place
And the loved one all together!—*Robert Browning*

Friendship is a disinterested commerce between equals; love, an abject intercourse between tyrants and slaves.—*Oliver Goldsmith*

When one is in love one begins by deceiving oneself, one ends by deceiving others. That is what the world calls romance.—*Oscar Wilde*

For though I know he loves me
Tonight my heart is sad
His kiss was not so wonderful
As all the dreams I had.—*Sara Teasdale*

One is very crazy when in love.—*Freud*

Love is a gross exaggeration of the difference between one person and everybody else.
    —*George Bernard Shaw*

The worst of having a romance is that it leaves one so unromantic.—*Oscar Wilde*

When first we met we did not guess
That Love would prove so hard a master.
    —*Robert Bridges*

To be in love is merely to be in a state of perceptual anesthesia—to mistake an ordinary young man for a Greek god or an ordinary young woman for a goddess.—*H. L. Mencken*

Lovers who have nothing to do but love each other are not really to be envied; love and nothing else very soon is nothing else.—*Walter Lippmann*

Great loves too must be endured.—*Coco Chanel*

> *You love me so much,*
> *you want to put me in your pocket.*
>
> *And I should die there smothered.*
>
> D. H. LAWRENCE

If two people love each other there can be no happy end to it.—*Ernest Hemingway*

Oh, life is a glorious cycle of song,
A medley of extemporanea;
And love is a thing that can never go wrong;
And I am Marie of Roumania.—*Dorothy Parker*

Love is the triumph of imagination over intelligence.—*H. L. Mencken*

And the lovers lie abed with all their griefs in their arms.—*Dylan Thomas*

There is hardly any activity, any enterprise, which is started with such tremendous hopes and expectations and yet which fails so regularly as love.
—*Erich Fromm*

Love is a universal migraine
A bright stain on the vision
Blotting out reason.—*Robert Graves*

One should always be wary of anyone who promises that their love will last longer than a weekend.—*Quentin Crisp*

Every young girl . . . tries to smother her first love in possessiveness. Oh what tears and rejection await the girl who imbues her first delicate match with fantasies of permanence, expecting that he at this gelatinous stage will fit with her in a finished puzzle for all the days.—*Gail Sheehy*

Great passions don't exist—they are liar's fantasies. What do exist are little loves that may last for a short or longer while.—*Anna Magnani*

There is one thing I would break up over, and that is if she caught me with another woman. I won't stand for that.—*Steve Martin*

I can see from your utter misery, from your eagerness to misunderstand each other, and from your thoroughly bad temper, that this is the real thing.—*Peter Ustinov*

People in love, it is well known, suffer extreme conceptual delusions; the most common of these being that other people find your condition as thrilling and eye-watering as you do yourselves.
    —*Julian Barnes*

She was a lovely girl. Our courtship was fast and furious—I was fast and she was furious.
    —*Max Kauffmann*

My boyfriend and I broke up. He wanted to get married, and I didn't want him to.—*Rita Rudner*

> *Doris, I think I'm in love with you.*
>
> *I mean, it's crazy.*
>
> *Really crazy!*
>
> *I mean I don't even know*
> *if you've read*
> *<u>The Catcher in the Rye</u>.*
>
> BERNARD SLADE

Told her I had always lived alone
And I probably always would,
And all I wanted was my freedom,
And she told me that she understood.
But I let her do some of my laundry
And she slipped a few meals in between,
The next thing I remember she was all moved in
And I was buying her a washing machine.
   —*Jackson Browne*

Kissing is a means of getting two people so close together that they can't see anything wrong with each other.—*René Yasenek*

To fall in love is to create a religion that has a fallible God.—*Jorge Luis Borges*

Love is simple to understand if you haven't got a mind soft and full of holes. It's a crutch, that's all and there isn't any one of us that doesn't need a crutch.—*Norman Mailer*

Love is mainly an affair of short spasms. If these spasms disappoint us, love dies. It is very seldom that it weathers the experience and becomes friendship.—*Jean Cocteau*

The happiest moments in any affair take place after the loved one has learned to accommodate the lover and before the maddening personality of either party has emerged like a jagged rock from the receding tides of lust and curiosity.
    —*Quentin Crisp*

To fall in love you have to be in the state of mind for it to take, like a disease.—*Nancy Mitford*

Love is the drug which makes sexuality palatable in popular mythology.—*Germaine Greer*

If you can stay in love for more than two years, you're *on* something.—*Fran Lebowitz*

In 1862,
as token of love and remorse,
Dante Gabriel Rossetti buried a
sheaf of original manuscript poems
with his dear departed wife,
Elizabeth Siddal.

In 1869,
having reconsidered
his romantic gesture,
Dante Gabriel Rossetti
exhumed his wife,
retrieved and subsequently
published the buried poems.

JON WINOKUR

A Brief and No Doubt Terribly Inaccurate History of Romantic Love

Romantic love is an illusion because it was created by entertainers. The poets, musicians, dancers, and painters—under the direct instructions of the Powers That Were—created lyrics, melodies, movements, paintings, sculptures, and the now-notorious etchings to praise the ruler's next, or most recent, sexual conquest with the same enthusiasm (and exaggeration) they used when documenting the Great One's military victories. The entire Old Testament book, Solomon's Song of Songs, seems bent on making King Solomon's physical passion high fashion. It was written around three thousand years ago, perhaps by Solomon himself or, by more likely, one of Solomon's temple poets.

It is, shall we say, unabashed in its celebration of the more erotic pleasures. God is mentioned only in passing, like the perfunctory grace murmured by ravenous diners after the food is already on the table.

If the Song of Songs were not part of the Old Testament, the Bible thumpers would have demanded its banning long ago. It is more an erotic miniseries than Bible lesson, with the characters Lover and Beloved exchanging passionate pleasantries—sort of an erotic *Can You Top This?**

---

*Actually, there seem to be three characters: Solomon; a pam-

*Illusion
is the first of all pleasures.*

<small>OSCAR WILDE</small>

pered beauty Solomon is just about to add or has recently added to his collection of wives; and another more secret object of Solomon's affection, most likely a man. The latter has fallen for the king in a Big Way, with all the passion and pathos of a 1930s torch singer. Here's an example of his/her heartbreak from Song of Songs 3:1–3 and 5:7—"All night long on my bed I looked for the one my heart loves; I looked for him but did not find him. I will get up now and go about the city, through its streets and squares; I will search for the one my heart loves. So I looked for him but did not find him. The watchmen found me as they made their rounds in the city. 'Have you seen the one my heart loves?' . . . They beat me, they bruised me; they took away my cloak, those watchmen of the walls!" Hardly the behavior—or the treatment—of the king's latest bride, one who is surrounded by handmaidens, and discourses the afternoon away on the tender pleasures of love.

Like their twentieth-century counterparts, the lovers use time-honored seduction techniques on each other:

Gifts (or at least *promises* of gifts) . . .

> We will make you earrings of gold, studded with silver. (1:11)

Flattery . . .

> Take me away with you—let us hurry! The king has brought me into his chambers. We rejoice and delight in you; we will praise your love more than wine. How right they are to adore you! (1:4)

> Your two breasts are like two fawns, like twin fawns of a gazelle that browse among the lilies. (4:5)

> How handsome you are, my lover! Oh, how charming! And our bed is verdant. (1:16)

Which leads inexorably to the main event . . .

> Like an apple tree among the trees of the forest is my lover among the young men. I delight to sit in his shade, and his fruit is sweet to my taste. He has taken me to the banquet hall, and his banner over me is love. Strengthen me with raisins, refresh me with apples, for I am faint with love. His left arm is under my head, and his right arm embraces me. (2:3–6)

> I slept but my heart was awake. Listen! My lover is knocking: "Open to me, my sister, my darling, my dove, my flawless one. My head is drenched with dew, my

> *He promised me earrings,*
> *but he only pierced my ears.*
>
> ARABIAN SAYING

hair with the dampness of the night." I have taken off my robe—must I put it on again? I have washed my feet—must I soil them again? My lover thrust his hand through the latch-opening; my heart began to pound for him. I arose to open for my lover, and my hands dripped with myrrh, my fingers with flowing myrrh, on the handles of the lock. (5:2–5)

Dripping with myrrh and dripping with metaphor, these could be passages from a romance novel published today. While the many seductive and erotic portrayals of true love in ancient literature, painting, and sculpture seem to prove that nothing really changes when it comes to human desire, significant elements have been incorporated into today's notion of romantic love that were unheard of until only a few centuries ago: monogamy, "till death do us part," equality of women, and average lifespans topping seventy years.

Prior to all that newfangled thinking and longer living, almost all marriages were arranged. From peasants to princesses, the *families*—not the participants—decided who would get hitched to whom.

These arrangements were often made at birth, and families would sometimes have an extra child especially to mate with an unspoken-for child in another family. To allow your parents to choose your spouse was accepted as a genetic inevitability—like eye color, balding pattern, or height.

These marriages often took place as soon as the couple was "ready for marriage"—specifically, when each had reached puberty. If you were able to reproduce, you were ready for marriage. In the Hebrew tradition, for example, a boy around thirteen would declare, "Today I am a man." His marriage followed shortly thereafter—sometimes on the same day.*

In such marriages, till death do us part was the rule. Considering, however, the pestilence, wars, epidemics, droughts, floods, and any number of wrathful gods who would wipe out entire populations just to make a minor point, even if you survived for very long, your spouse probably wouldn't. Till death do

---

*Mary was probably twelve or thirteen when she had Jesus. She wasn't married to Joseph when the news of her pregnancy came, but merely betrothed, which usually happened by the age of twelve.

> *In olden times sacrifices*
> *were made at the altar—*
> *a practice which is still continued.*
>
> HELEN ROWLAND

you part, then, was usually a five- to six-year contract. With an average lifespan of about thirty-five, the husband or wife who lived to that ripe old age could have five or more domestic partners.

Nobility had arranged marriages, too, but nobility (naturally) had a loophole. The loopholes went by the name of mistresses, concubines, courtesans, lovers, palace guards, and, of course, multiple wives. Solomon dismissed—but acknowledged the presence of—his erotic entourage as he wooed his latest prize:

> Sixty queens there may be, and eighty concubines, and virgins beyond number; but my dove, my perfect one, is unique, the only daughter of her mother, the favorite of the one who bore her. The maidens

saw her and called her blessed; the queens
and concubines praised her. (6:8–9)

This arrangement was described by Oscar Hammerstein II in *The King and I*:

> A woman must be like a blossom,
> with honey for just one man.
> A man must be like a honey bee,
> and gather all he can.
> To fly from blossom to blossom,
> the honey bee must be free.
> But blossom must not ever fly,
> from bee to bee to bee!

In theory, the queens and concubines remained faithful, but in practice, well, what the honey bee doesn't know won't hurt him.

The word *court* originally meant a walled space in front of the house where chickens and other livestock were kept. The wall was a sign of wealth and power—and offered some protection from nosy-greedy-jealous neighbors. As the power and wealth of the powerful and wealthy grew, the courts became larger and larger, becoming covered spaces. Eventually, the great hall where the powerful brokered became known as the court. As it was also the ruler's job to dispense justice, royal courts became the basis for our courts of law today (where the majority of married couples will end up for divorce proceedings).

Naturally, the courts of the rich and powerful attracted rich and powerful wannabes, hangers on, and anyone the ruler found amusing. Hence, *courtiers* and

> *We declare that love cannot exist*
> *between two people*
> *who are married to each other.*
>
> *For lovers give to each other freely,*
> *under no compulsion;*
> *married people are in duty bound*
> *to give in to each other's desires.*
>
> MARIE, COUNTESS OF CHAMPAGNE
> 1174

courtesans, raising flattery and pleasure to world-class levels. Among the courtiers and courtesans, of course, would be some dangerous liaisons. Among these, romance was high on the list. The members of the court wooed with what they knew—praise and presents—which led to the word *courtship.*

All of these are French words because romantic flattery reached a peak in the courts of France. Troubadours were hired to sing songs of love, lust, and longing to any *objet d'desire.* Fashion was used to attract romance. Satin clothing, lace, high heels, elaborate wigs, and jewelry, jewelry everywhere. (The women dressed nicely, too.)

The end result of all this courtship was, occasionally, one of those till-death-do-us-part marriages. What a concept! Getting *married* to the person you feel passionate about. What would the French think of next? Although the custom met with limited acceptance, by the time of the French Revolution—and especially after—it became a more popular pursuit.

The United States in the 1800s became a hotbed of select-your-own-spouse activity. Any number of people left the Old World and its old customs because they wanted to have some say in who their spousal roommate might be—and even more left to escape the mate selected by fate (that is, their parents): "I am not exactly sure *what* I'm looking for, but I *know* it is not *that.*"

Another significant difference between then and now is the way in which women were viewed. Inexplicably, throughout the history of what we call Western civilization* women have been treated appallingly. In biblical times, for the most part, they were viewed as one step above cattle. The man *owned* his wives, and listed them among an inventory of his possessions. Well into the nineteenth century, women had no rights, could not own property, and could not enter into contractual agreements. The reason prostitution is the world's oldest profession is that the *only* thing a woman who was not under the "protection" (and the thumb) of a man *could* sell was her body. In legal or criminal disputes between men

*Mahatma Ghandi was once asked what he thought of Western civilization. He replied, "It would be a good idea."

> *Perhaps in time*
> *the so-called Dark Ages*
> *will be thought of*
> *as including our own.*

G. C. LICHTENBERG

and women, men always prevailed.

To wealthy families, women were such a burden that the father offered money to any man who agreed to take the daughter away and spend a fraction of her own inheritance taking care of her. In *Taming of the Shrew,* when Petruchio arrives in town, he proclaims,

> I come to wive it wealthily in Padua;
> If wealthily, then happily in Padua.

It was not the daughter, but the size of her dowry that aroused the passions of eligible men. In poorer families, the solution was often more direct—excess female children were murdered at birth. Children who were not able to start working in the fields—as most boys were—within a few years of birth were dispensed with.

When Thomas Jefferson wrote, "all men are created equal," he meant *men*, not women. The year 1776 was not the year of independence for American women. Women were arrested for smoking cigarettes as late as 1904, and Margaret Sanger was jailed in 1916 for teaching birth control. As hard as it is to believe, women did not have the right to vote in the United States until 1920. Even more astonishing: in Canada women did not have the right to vote until 1948.

In romance and marriage, the concept that women are equal to men is only a few decades old. A great many people in this country still haven't heard the news.

Another radical difference between then and now is lifespan. In the past three to four centuries the average lifespan has nearly doubled. Reaching thirty-five was once considered an accomplishment; today pushing seventy is commonplace. Thanks to indoor plumbing (which took septic waste away) and improved transportation (which made fresh fruits and vegetables available all year), combined with the three A's of modern medicine (antibiotics, anesthetics, and antiseptics), "happily ever after" has become a long, long, *long* time. Whereas "till death do us part" meant five to six years in the Middle Ages, it means—for the average twenty-one-year-old embarking on this adventure for the first time—more than half a century.

But enough on why romance isn't working. Let's focus instead on the solution.

*All hatred
driven hence,
The soul recovers
radical innocence
And learns at last
that it is self-delighting,
Self-appeasing, self-affrighting,
And that
its own sweet will
is Heaven's will.*

WILLIAM BUTLER YEATS

The Solution to Loving and Being Loved Is Right under (and over, and around, and Including) Your Nose

There's an old story about a brainstorming session called by God to discuss plans for the creation of the world.

"Nearly everything's taken care of," God observed, looking over the vast blueprint for Earth and all its inhabitants, "except we still have a few very important decisions to make. One of the most important is 'Where do we hide humanity's true self?'" This was important because, at a previous planning session, it was decided that one of the games people would play on Earth—just to keep them from getting bored—would be Hide-and-Go-Seek. God would hide certain things on Earth—such as humanity's true self—and it would be up to human beings to find them.

This question prompted a flurry of suggestions. "Let's hide it on the highest mountain!" one of the architectural archangels recommended.

"No," said God, "someday human beings will climb the highest mountains and they'll find it."

"Let's hide it on the dark side of the moon!" one of the seraphim suggested.

"No," God said, "one day humanity will explore the moon—even the dark side—and the true self will be discovered."

> *I was told that the Chinese said*
> *they would bury me by the Western Lake*
> *and build a shrine to my memory.*
>
> *I have some slight regret*
> *that this did not happen,*
> *as I might have become a god,*
> *which would have been*
> *very <u>chic</u> for an atheist.*
>
> BERTRAND RUSSELL

"Let's put it at the bottom of the deepest ocean," offered a cherub.

"That's the best hiding place so far," said God, "but some day humans will even plumb the depths of the deepest oceans and find the *Titanic* of their true selves." God's little pun was met with polite laughter and a few celestial groans. "Besides," God continued, "we don't want all humanity to find their true selves at the same time. Then the game would be over forever. That's no fun."

A great peace settled on the heavenly conference room. Eventually, the voice of a timid but thoughtful angel broke the silence.

"Why don't we hide humanity's true self inside each and every human being?"

"Excellent!" proclaimed God. "Hide it in plain sight. Put it in the most obvious place of all. It will take them *forever* to find it inside themselves." God, who loves games, chuckled with delight.

"If it's going to be all that difficult, shouldn't we provide some clues?" asked an angel who was particularly fond of Earth.

"Yes," said God, "I suppose that would be only fair. In fact, we'll have *all* the great teachers of the true self tell humanity precisely where it is." God turned to the right. "Jesus."

"Yes, Dad?"

"Why don't you say something like this when you're down there: 'The kingdom of heaven is within you,' or 'the kingdom of God is within you,'—something like that? Where else would the true self reside than in the kingdom of God?"

"Sure, Dad," Jesus replied, writing in his notebook. "I'll say it in Luke 17:21."

"Isn't that a little obvious?" asked one of the game-loving angels. "I mean, isn't that *giving* it away?"

"No," said God, "on Earth only the hummingbird has a shorter attention span than the human being. Most humans won't even hear it. Those who do hear it, and believe it, and discover it's true, will most likely forget it."

"Do you think we should give humans a few more memory chips?" an electrical engineering angel asked.

God pondered this for some time and finally remarked, "I don't think so. Maybe. Let's see how they do with the current allotment. But, just to be

> *Men talk of "finding God,"*
> *but no wonder it is difficult;*
> *He is hidden in that*
> *darkest hiding-place,*
> *your heart.*
>
> *You yourself are a part of him.*
>
> CHRISTOPHER MORLEY

fair, let's give them another clue. Jesus, add to your statement about the kingdom of God being within something like 'seek ye first the kingdom of God and all these things shall be added unto you.'"

"Sure, Dad," Jesus said, pulling out his notebook again. "I'll say that in Matthew 6:33 and Luke 12:31."

"There," God said, "are we all agreed?" There were murmurs of approval and delight. The angels couldn't wait to see how much *fun* human beings would have playing the Hide-and-Go-Seek-Yourself game. "Great! Let's break for lunch—it's on me. Diet Ambrosia for all!" There were general cheers and hurrahs from the satisfied but famished angels.

Here is where they usually put the fade-out in

this story. It's as though this were the last major decision to be made. Most people assume that the cosmic construction crew got to work and six days later, there was Earth. The storytellers usually fail to relate what happened in the *afternoon* session. Another very important decision was yet to be made.

"Human beings have an in-built desire to love and to be loved," God said, "to care for and to be cared for; to support and be supported; to please and be pleased. Where shall we hide each human being's true love?"

"Begging your pardon, God," said the angel in charge of budgeting Earth, "but do humans really *need* any more love? After all, we are sending down legions of angels—at enormous expense—who have nothing to do but love and protect human beings. These angels are, it is well-known, exceedingly lovable. Then there is all the wonderful *energy* flowing in and around everything—what do you call it . . . ?"

"Life," God answered. "Or life force, spirit, cosmic energy, creative intelligence—it has a lot of names."

"Yeah, that," the CPA cherub said. "This energy seems to be loving; in fact, it seems to be *ostentatiously* loving."

"Well, that's because it *is*," God reminded the budget-conscious angel.

"Do you have any idea what it costs to maintain this energy, every day, all the time?"

"Yes," God said with a knowing smile, "I know, I know."

"Then we have all the emissaries you will be sending to Earth on one loving mission after another. The travel budget alone is astounding. And we have

> *You must believe in God,*
> *in spite of what the clergy say.*
>
> BENJAMIN JOWETT

to amortize the cost of blessings, grace, miracles. Take your son Jesus, for example . . ."

"That won't be very expensive," said God. "A few robes, a couple of pairs of sandals, a donkey . . . not much."

"But there's the *resurrection*," sighed the cost-cutting angel in exasperation. His eyes would have rolled heavenward were the angel not already in heaven. "Do you know how *expensive* a resurrection is? Why, the paperwork alone . . ."

"Yes, I know, I know . . ."

"And then there is *you*," the fiscally responsible angel said, checking his Earth Construction Cost Analysis; "it says that you will *personally* dwell within each human on Earth!"

"If that's where we put the kingdom of God, where else am I supposed to dwell?"

"But have you considered the *duplication* costs?"

"Haven't these already been approved?" asked God.

"Yes, yes, I'm just trying to avoid redundancy. Certainly if you are inside each human being, loving them from the inside out, can't they just love you back and let that be enough loving?"

"Humans loving humans is like bananas on cereal," God said. "It's certainly not necessary, but it is nice."

"There were a lot of nice things we didn't include—television without commercials, Häagen Dazs as a health food, honest politicians, televangelists who have at least *skimmed* the Bible . . ."

"Oh, the unkind things they do in my name!" said Jesus, shaking his head.

"You agreed to be crucified by those on Earth," God reminded him.

"Yes, but I didn't think it would be like *that*," said Jesus.

"Always read the small print in the contract, son," God reminded him.

"If I may continue," the financial angel said.

"Please," said God.

". . . eyes in the back of human heads plus one on top, a tropical climate for New York City—the list of unfundable niceties goes on and on . . ."

"Let's put humans loving humans into the category of *very* nice, then," said God, exercising his godly prerogative.

"You mean like songbirds, sunsets, and portable

> *It is the test of a good religion*
> *whether you can joke about it.*
>
> G. K. CHESTERTON

CD players?" the CPAngel asked, reviewing the very nice list. "Spacious skies; amber waves of grain, purple mountain majesties; above the fruited plain . . ."

"Yeah," God said. "That list."

"Very well," the CPAngel (who was always secretly pleased when God bumped something wonderful up to a higher budgetary category) said, "we'll put it in here—right under colors, music, and forgiveness."

"So," said God returning to his original question, "who would be a human's perfect human lover?"

"What are the qualities of a perfect lover for humans?" an angel asked.

"Good question," said God. "Ideas?" he asked the assembled throng.

"The lover would have to know the beloved well," suggested one angel. "Likes, dislikes, wants, preferences—and then be willing to supply the good rather than the bad."

"Yes, and the lover would have to know *when* the beloved wanted the preferred good," another angel added, "and how much, and for how long."

"They would have to be together all the time," a third angel suggested; "that way when one or another of them wanted something, the other one would be always there to provide it."

"And this would mean that they would have to be able to live together, sleep together, eat together, and bathe together. They would have to be together during sickness and in health, in good times and bad, till death do them part."

"It would be nice if they both got into movie theaters for the same price," one of the more practical angels suggested.

"Yes," said God, "these are very good characteristics of ideal lovers. Who, then, is each human being's ideal lover?"

A flurry of suggestions cascaded in:

"Their soulmate!"

"The one who says 'I will.'"

"Their star-crossed lover!"

"Marky Mark!"

"Their Valentine!"

"No, no, no," God said at last, "you're all considerably off track. Think *deeper* on this; think *practically* about love. That's something *we* can do that

> *The world embarrasses me,*
> *and I cannot dream*
> *That this watch exists*
> *and has no watchmaker.*
>
> VOLTAIRE

human beings don't seem to be capable of. It's our job, then, to provide the right answer, and to leave lots of clues about that answer all over the Earth."

Another silence descended on the heavenly conference hall. Some angels went into deep reverie. Eventually, the thoughtful but timid angel who had suggested that humanity's true self be hidden within each human being spoke.

"The answer is simple," he said. All of heaven turned to listen to his words of wisdom. "We'll just make sure that every human is a Siamese twin."

"Closer," said God, "but not exactly there."

"And *very, very* expensive," said the CPAngel.

"Dad," said Jesus, looking through the notebook he was preparing for his earthly journey, "when in

Matthew 19:19 and Mark 12:31 I repeat your commandment 'love your neighbor as yourself,' it doesn't just mean to love your neighbor. Aren't you also telling people not to love any other human *more* than themselves?"

"Very good, Jesus," God said. "Just as 'the kingdom of God is within you,' it is quite clear, but will be astonishingly misunderstood. Human beings must learn to love themselves *first*, and *then* they will be able to love their neighbor. They won't be able to help it, in fact."

"I don't remember 'love your neighbor as yourself,' being one of the ten commandments," said an angel.

"It's not, but it is one of the two commandments that form the foundation for all the Old Testament teachings," God said. "Jesus, what do you say at Matthew 22:37–40?" asked God.

"About the same thing I say at Mark 12:28–31 and Luke 10:25–27," Jesus said, looking through his notebook.

"The one at Matthew 22:36–40 reads:

> "'Teacher, which is the greatest commandment in the Law?' Jesus replied: "'Love the Lord your God with all your heart and with all your soul and with all your mind.' This is the first and greatest commandment. And the second is like it: 'Love your neighbor as yourself.' All the Law and the Prophets hang on these two commandments.'"

"Why does it say that the second commandment is like the first?" an angel asked.

> *There is a Law that man should*
> *love his neighbor as himself.*
>
> *In a few years it should be*
> *as natural to mankind as*
> *breathing or the upright gait;*
> *but if he does not learn it*
> *he must perish.*
>
> ALFRED ADLER

"Although I certainly like being loved," God said, "the reason humans are asked to love God is that *loving feels good*. If they're loving me with all their heart, soul, and mind, they are immersed in love and, therefore, in good feelings. The second commandment is like it because . . . Jesus, why don't you take this one?"

"One of the things that can interfere with loving God is hating what's on Earth. If humans are preoccupied with hating themselves and each other, they will be filled with hate and not love, which is neither enjoyable nor productive. In other words, if you are a human being and you're loving God, yourself, and your neighbor as yourself, then life is bound to be primarily loving."

"My boy!" said God proudly.

"Are you saying, God, that the best human lover for each individual human is himself or herself?" asked an angel.

"Each human is a lover and beloved in one?" asked another.

"Precisely," said God. "First, love God as you understand God to be; yourself second; and then everyone else. Those are the rules for a happy, productive, satisfying human life."

"That won't cost much," said the cost-conscious angel, "in fact, if they do that, this Earth venture could be nearly self-sustaining."

"Does this agree with what you will be teaching, Moses?" God asked.

"Fine, fine," said Moses.

"Confucius?" asked God.

"Yes, yes," Confucius nodded.

"Buddha?" God asked.

"Ah, yes," said Buddha.

"Krishna?"

"Of course," said Krishna.

"Mohammed?"

"Certainly, yes," said Mohammed.

"Tony Robbins?" asked God.

"He's out making another infomercial," said one of the angels.

"Oh, that's right," said God.

"But I think Tony would agree, too."

> *Love is a metaphysical gravity.*
>
> R. BUCKMINSTER FULLER

It was getting on toward evening. The heavenly bodies gathered 'round the place in time and space earmarked for the construction of Earth. They looked into the void that would soon be separated into the heavens and the earth.

"Will the human beings practice what we teach them and be happy," one of the Earth emissaries asked in a soft voice, "or do something else and be miserable?"

"Each human being has that choice in each moment of human existence—it's that free-will clause we are experimenting with."

"Will most human beings choose to love God, love themselves, and love their neighbors?"

"If they accept God for what *they* perceive God

to be and not what other people proclaim God to be, then loving God is easy," said God. "They will then have all the loving they need to take care of themselves, and to give to others from the abundance."

"Will most human beings choose to do so?"

"Most human beings will choose to do it at least some of the time," said God.

"Eventually, what choice will most human beings make most of the time?"

"That's the end of the story," said God. "Do you really want to know the end of the story?"

"No, I guess not. It's more fun to watch and see what happens."

"I agree," said God. "That's why even I chose to not know the ending myself."

Do right
<u>for your own sake</u>,
and be happy
in knowing
that your <u>neighbor</u>
will certainly share
in the benefits
resulting.

MARK TWAIN

Self-Love vs. Selfishness

Selfishness—in its negative sense—means, "I love me, and only me, and the hell with you." People who are selfish in the extreme are, in fact, *sociopathic*—on the way to the store to buy a bag of cookies, these people will run you over, because stopping for you would have deprived them of the cookies one minute longer.

This is obviously *not* the sort of self-love I am promoting. While self-love certainly does not mean pleasing others at the expense of yourself (unless you choose to do so), it also does not mean one should please oneself at others' expense.

Putting your needs first—a fundamental tenet of self-love—is not only common sense; it is also essential if you want to do for others. If you do not, say, fulfill your need to sleep because you want to "sacrifice yourself" for the good of others, within a few days you will collapse and others will have to do for you. And prior to your collapse, your fatigued doing may become another's undoing.

So it is in all relationships—if you take care of your needs and wants, being with others is more enjoyable and productive. In fact, for most people, self-love makes one *less* selfish.

Another reason self-love has a bad name is that people confuse it with the extremes of self-indulgence epitomized by King Louis XIV and his "chalet" at Versailles; Howard Hughes, who—as Ted Morgan explained—indulged his madness (and, consequently, his misery), "like a man who not only thinks he is

> *Selfishness is not
> living as one wishes to live,
> it is asking others
> to live as one wishes to live.*
>
> OSCAR WILDE

Napoleon, but hires an army to prove it"; or Stalin, who was such a self-indulgent mass murderer that he could coolly proclaim: "the death of one person is a tragedy—the death of a million is a statistic." Excessive self-indulgence is the cause of statistics in world history, which are the cause of excessive self-indulgence's well-deserved unsavory reputation.

Fortunately, extreme self-indulgence is usually met with rapid and sometimes fatal enervation. Unfortunately, it doesn't happen in all cases. These are the ones that tend to become celebrated.

Another excess cited when criticizing the term *self-love* is complete self-absorption. With this, at least no harm is done to anyone except those whose attentions are spurned (or, more accurately, ignored) by the self-absorbee. When the self-absorption is with one's physical beauty (a temptation which, alas, I have never been presented), it is often called *narcissism*. The name comes from the Greek legend of Narcissus, who was so taken by his own reflection in a pool that he abandoned both his male and female lovers for his own, albeit considerable, reflected glory.

Almost everyone I've encountered would profit from at least a little more self-kindness, self-caring, and self-pampering.

Yes, there are those who have a bravado which *appears* to be megalomanical, narcissistic, or excessively self-centered, but almost invariably this is just the hard shell that covers a quivering mass of insecurities, self-doubt, and often self-hatred. A good dose of self-love makes these people more loving of others.

Of the handful of people I've met in my time* who have a genuine excess of self-love, most were certified sociopaths and the rest were studying diligently for certification. One thing could be said for all of them, however—they wouldn't be caught dead reading a book on the subject of self-love.** Someone with too much self-love reading a book on self-help is like Queen Elizabeth II reading a book on how to be a queen. She is so busy *being* a queen,

*Which, in the year 2050, will span more than a century.

**Well, one of the sociopaths I know would probably read this book, but only because he hates me so much. The subject matter itself, by another author, would never appeal to him. Like most sociopaths, he keeps much better track of his enemies and potential enemies than he does of his friends.

> *If egotism means
> a terrific interest in one's self,
> egotism is absolutely essential
> to efficient living.*
>
> ARNOLD BENNETT

she has no time to read about it. Those who suffer from a dangerous excess of self-love won't be reading this book—or any other self-help book—because it simply does not occur to them that their self is in need of any help.

I consider this good news, indeed. If you have read this far in the book, you are almost certainly not one of the sociopaths. In other words, if you are reading this book, you could almost certainly use a bit more self-love.

*Selfness is
an essential fact of life.*

*The thought of nonselfness,
precise sameness,
is terrifying.*

LEWIS THOMAS

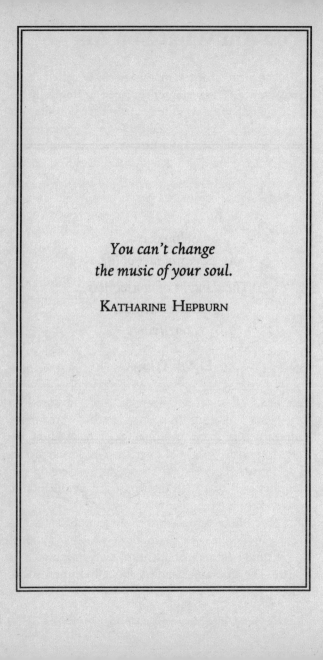

You can't change
the music of your soul.

KATHARINE HEPBURN

You Am What You Am

The next chapter in this book is called "Self-Acceptance." This chapter is placed strategically before that chapter to demonstrate that you have *no choice,* for the most part, *except* self-acceptance.

You are condemned to the magnificence that you already *are* (with a few misunderstood eccentricities and a couple of warts thrown in). You might as well enjoy it. In fact, you might as well make a living from it. But we are now several chapters down the line. This is our chapter on biology.

Not biology generally, but a specific branch of biology—genetics.

At that grand moment—the most important in your history—Mom and Dad went skinny dipping in the gene pool and conceived you, unique in all the world (unless you have an identical twin). Contained within the chromosome soup of the fertilized egg was everything necessary to determine your eventual height, eye color, skin color, balding pattern, and, of course, gender. Also encoded into the genetic make-up, as science has discovered more recently, was your personality, predisposition toward a certain weight at a certain age, sexual preference, innate talents, and a tendency to develop certain diseases at certain times in your life, including, most likely, the one that will kill you.

This information comes from a number of scientific sources, the most dramatic of which was a long-term study of sets of identical twins separated at birth. The question bandied about freshmen socio-

> *We are all omnibuses*
> *in which our ancestors ride,*
> *and every now and then*
> *one of them sticks his head out*
> *and embarrasses us.*
>
> OLIVER WENDELL HOLMES

logy classes for decades has been: "Which is more important, heredity or environment?" Identical twins separated at birth—who are identical genetically but with different environments (sometimes radically different)—would answer the question scientifically. If twins from the same set had different personalities, then environment was more important than heredity. If the twins had pretty much the same personalities, then it would be heredity over environment. If the results were mixed—some similarities and some differences—the answer would be a little heredity and a little environment.

As it turns out, the twins were nearly as identical in personality as they were in genetic structure. While they certainly had individual differences—a tendency to give to others might manifest in becoming a nurse for one and running a charity for the other—the basic personality was almost identical.

When I use the word *personality* I am not speaking superficially, as in "she has a nice personality," or "he's got personality-plus." I am referring to all those characteristics that differentiate *us* from others. When we describe a "self" that begins to be cosmic, spiritual, or transcendental, we see that this same self exists in many—if not all—people. When we talk about *our* self, we usually talk about what makes us unique, different, special. What we define as ourselves, as in the phrase "I'm learning to love myself," psychologists would probably refer to as the personality.

The personality* determines not just how we present ourselves to the world, but also how we fundamentally *perceive* the world. Do we see the world as a good or bad place? According to psychologists, that's part of the personality. Do we have a tendency to respond to disappointment with hurt or anger? That, too, is the personality. Our sense of self-worth and self-esteem is found in the personality. How much we worry (or not) is part of the personality. The degree to which we feel guilt, and the way in which we resolve guilt is in the personality. The amount of fear we feel? Personality. The list goes on and on.

*The word comes from the Greek *persona*, which was the mask and amplified mouthpiece used in Greek plays to differentiate one character from another, and to amplify and project the actor's words.

> *Man's main task in life*
> *is to give birth to himself,*
> *to become what he potentially is.*
>
> *The most important*
> *product of his effort*
> *is his own personality.*
>
> ERICH FROMM

Naturally, extremes in the environment in which we are raised can alter us for good or for ill. But for the most part, most of us (that is, the majority of us who read and write books with titles such as *LOVE 101*) grew up within a normal range of environmental shocks and satisfactions.

If we can change our personality no more easily than we can change our eye color, then the way we approach ourselves and learn to love ourselves may be considerably different than the way we thought (or have been taught) to do.

It may be much, much, *much* easier.

Say, for example, after much poking about in your environmental past (that is, your parents, teachers, siblings, home life, what you saw on TV, the books you read, the friends you had while grow-ing up, and so on), you discovered a memory of a significant disappointment when you were three years old. It was this event, you now claim after much deliberation and inner investigation, that ac-counts for your being so easily discouraged today, and this is why you have accomplished far less than your true potential dictates.

Using one of the psychological models that have been increasingly popular over the past cen-tury, to do more *now*, you would have to go back to *then*, and somehow "resolve" the conflict that occurred when you were three. This can take a lot of time, work, and money. After all that, how do you know whether or not you've really gotten all the disappointment resolved? What if you find that this disappointment only points to an earlier trauma?

I know people who have been "working on themselves" for *decades*. Most have accomplished nothing more than giving the notion of working on oneself a bad name. Talk about self-indulgence! But, then, I was one of them. (More on me later.)

Let's explore the same phenomenon of being easily discouraged from a genetic rather than an environmental point of view.

You have noticed that you become easily dis-couraged and, therefore, have not achieved all that you've wanted. You remember a time when you were three years old and a childhood disappoint-ment caused you to become discouraged. From a *genetic* point of view, the evaluation is simple: "I must have a genetic predisposition to be easily

> *Breed is stronger than pasture.*
>
> GEORGE ELIOT

discouraged. I remember feeling disappointed and becoming discouraged as early as three."

As you can't go back and fix your genes, you return to today and ask, "If I want to get more things done, what can I do with my genetic predisposition toward discouragement?"

This is a question you can do something about *today*, right now. You can *consciously compensate* for a tendency toward discouragement in any number of ways—affirmations, regularly scheduled pep talks (from yourself or others), learning to keep doing in spite of discouragement, and other techniques we will be exploring later in this book.

The notion that our environment caused some deep psychological scar, a scar that must be healed, rather than a genetic toss of the dice that includes all the greatness and limitations in our make-up, has been a fundamental barrier to loving ourselves. We fail to do the most important self-loving act of all—accept ourselves—and *then* learn to work with our accepted assets *and* liabilities.

We accept that we are a certain height, our hair a certain texture, our eyes a certain color. We accept these—we may not like them, but we accept them. We do not for a *moment* pretend that if we explored the traumas of our childhood we would grow three inches, our hair would become wavy, or our eyes turn stunning blue. No, we are as tall, wavy, and blue as nature made us, and if it's important enough to us, we get busy compensating for what we got. We buy elevator shoes, get our hair permed, and order a pair of contact lenses in Brad Pitt blue.

Can you see how absurd it's been to look at behavioral patterns in ourselves and try to go back in time and change them? You am what you am, and what you am was determined when you was first am'd—the moment your mother's genes and father's genes were thrown together in that great turn of the genetic roulette wheel. When the ball settled, there you were. To pretend you can somehow go back in time, shake the table, and make the ball land elsewhere—well, talk about discouraging. And impossible.

More about this in the next chapter on acceptance. For now, allow me to close this chapter by making a personal observation on our genetic heritage.

> *Most people are <u>on</u> the world,*
> *not in it—having no conscious*
> *sympathy or relationship*
> *to anything about them—*
> *undiffused, separate, and rigidly alone*
> *like marbles of polished stone,*
> *touching but separate.*
>
> JOHN MUIR

I'd like to challenge the concept that we were somehow placed *on* the earth by spiritual beings or flying saucers, rather than organically growing *from* the earth, like flowers, birds, and Lhasa apsos. Many people believe that because, as human beings, we don't personally relate to nature, we can't consider ourselves one of its marvels.

But we *are* marvelous, not just for what we *do*, but for what we *are*. Consider the genetic wonders of the plant world—plants do all they do without ever being taught. Contained within a single seed is all the knowledge a plant needs to grow into whatever it is—a flower, a carrot, a pomegranate, a towering oak.

Insects do all that they do without being taught. Contained in a microscopic egg abandoned by its parents before birth is the information to grow, feed, metamorphose, migrate thousands of miles, build communities, and reproduce.

Imagine how much more elaborate and spectacular our genetic make-up is than plants and insects. We are, of course, evolutionarily superior to plants and insects, but we often think of ourselves as *exceptionally* superior—as though we were accidentally dropped from our spiritual baby carriage on high, and fell onto a hostile planet with which we have nothing in common. Because we are spiritual, we begin to associate with the higher levels of intelligence a little *too* much—to the point of ignoring and abandoning our natural, earthly, genetic roots.

It's a shame. There's such wisdom, magnificence, and mystery in nature—and *we* are a part of it. Yes, we will always aspire toward more—that's what human beings do.

But while we aspire toward greater and greater, why not also delight in how great we already are? And, if we can't quite bring ourselves to relish it, let's at least accept it.

And, even if you don't accept a word of this chapter as true—even if we are what we are entirely because of environment—the first and most important step to loving oneself is *still* self-acceptance.

I cannot love anyone if I hate myself.

That is the reason why
we feel so
extremely uncomfortable
in the presence of people
who are noted for
their special virtuousness,
for they radiate
an atmosphere
of the torture
they inflict on themselves.

That is not a virtue but a vice.

CARL JUNG

Self-Acceptance

When we fail to accept ourselves, *all* of ourselves—the good, the bad, the ugly, and the beautiful—it is very difficult to get *anything* done, especially loving ourselves.

Not accepting ourselves is like receiving some sort of game as a gift—but, rather than having fun playing it, we try to play a *different* game using the elements of the game we were given. It's hard to play Trivial Pursuit with a Monopoly set, Parcheesi on a backgammon board, or poker with a Nintendo Ninja Warrior cartridge.

This lack of acceptance seems to stem from our desire to fit in, to get along, to be "the same." So we use the model of an "average" whatever we happen to be (average girl, average boy, average child of a coal miner, average student at a certain school, and so on) to torture into normality any portion of ourselves that doesn't seem to "fit in."

This, obviously, destroys our uniqueness. It lops off the best and the worst of what we are.

Ironically, we generally admire, emulate, and even adore people because of their uniqueness. Their special qualities—not their run-of-the-mill-just-like-everyone-else-qualities—attract us to others, be they movie stars, mentors, or best friends. In our own lives, however, we too often follow the pack and suppress all those marvelous eccentricities that make us—as they say in show business—*marketable*. We condemn our specialness and join the mediocre in yet another lukewarm chorus of "The Bland

> *The "what should be" never did exist,*
> *but people keep trying to live up to it.*
>
> *There is no "what should be,"*
> *there is only what is.*
>
> LENNY BRUCE

Played On."

If we truly accept our negative *and* our positive, we can do something with them—we can exploit the positive and compensate for the negative.

If you want to be a model and your face is exceptional, flaunt it. If you want to be a model and your face is not exceptional, then you had better be sure that your body—or some other marketable aspect of yourself—more than compensates for it. If you like to write fiction but can't seem to sustain a plot longer than a short story, don't try to sell what you're doing as a short story; say it's "a novel of economical style in the tradition of *The Bridges of Madison County.*" If you like to exercise, become a personal trainer. If you don't like to exercise, hire a personal trainer (or become a writer). It all begins with acceptance.

Acceptance is the step *before* you even evaluate whether something is positive or negative. Acceptance is simply seeing something for what it is and saying, "This is what it is." "I tend to get angry when someone lets me down." There is no need to apply right or wrong, good or bad, useful or limiting. Simply see it for what it is, and accept it.

Postpone the determination as to whether each characteristic that makes up *you* is a benefit or a detriment. For now, simply accept everything about yourself—including and especially those things you would only divulge to your best friend (and only if very drunk), or would only admit to a trusted therapist (and only if you were paying a lot of money).

There is no human quality that can't be compensated for (a concept I find more productive than *change)*, and no characteristic that can't be used to get more of what you really want.

Harry Cohn, who founded Columbia Pictures, had a mean streak and a terrible temper. He was angry so often that someone once asked him, "Don't you have an ulcer yet?" Cohn responded, "I don't get ulcers; I give 'em." Consequently, Harry Cohn, the person, did not have a good reputation. He was the butt of any number of jokes and anecdotes, including, literally, this one:

Cohn told the writer/director Joseph Mankiewicz that a film he was making was too long.

"How do you know it's too long?" Mankiewicz asked.

"Because during the screening my fanny started

> *If you accept your limitations*
> *you go beyond them.*
>
> BRENDAN FRANCIS

to itch," Cohn answered. "When a picture gets too long, my fanny itches."

As Mankiewicz later said to friends, "It's frightening to consider that the taste of the American public is wired to Harry Cohn's ass."

When Cohn died, someone asked Red Skelton why, if Cohn was such a hated man in Hollywood, did so many people come to his funeral. "It's the first law of show business," Skelton answered. "Give people what they want and they'll come out for it."

There is not a shred of evidence to indicate that Harry Cohn ever tried to control his temper. What he did do, however, was compensate for it. His compensation: he loved what creative people did. "I worship creativity," he once said, "it's my religion." If someone brought him a good idea, a good performer, or a good script, Cohn backed it. It didn't matter whether the creator had a name in the business or not. If he thought a person—writer, director, producer, composer, cinematographer, editor, or performer—was talented, he or she got a chance (under Cohn's *strict* supervision, of course).

One of the most famous and successful opportunities Cohn gave another was to Frank Capra. Capra had the notion that it was the *director* and not the *producer* who should have the final say in what the finished picture should be. This is now an accepted idea, but in Hollywood of the early 1930s, the director was expendable and interchangeable. In Hollywood of the 1930s, the producer ruled the roost. Cohn was willing to step aside and give Capra his chance. The result? *It Happened One Night, You Can't Take It With You,* and *Mr. Smith Goes to Washington,* among others.

Capra, however, had to work within Cohn's system. Capra, who had something of a hot temper himself, controlled it, and let Cohn vent his rage on every subject under the sun. As long as Capra got what he needed to make the films he wanted, he considered controlling his temper a reasonable trade. He also found ways of not just overcoming Cohn's seemingly arbitrary regulations at the studio, but using his own creativity (which he had in great abundance) to turn what most considered a limitation into an asset.

For example, at one point Cohn decided that the directors on the Columbia lot were making "too

> *The most important thing*
> *is to be whatever you are*
> *without shame.*
>
> ROD STEIGER

many takes." He limited the number of takes a director could make to three per scene. "If you can't make it in three takes, you're out!"

Rather than complain to Cohn that more than three takes were sometimes necessary to make a good picture, Capra found a loophole in Cohn's edict. Cohn didn't say *how long* each take could be. Capra would begin a take, the actors would do the scene, and Capra would let the film run as the actors quickly returned to their original positions and did the scene again. Capra and his nimble actors were able to squeeze four, five, even six takes into a single technical "take."

This, Capra noticed, had the effect of keeping the actors up, the mood breezy, the dialogue natural—a tone that became one of Capra's trademarks—and it all began as a creative way of compensating for what every other director on the lot considered an insurmountable limitation.

It is not until we accept our limitations (Cohn's anger or Capra's three takes), and our talents (Cohn's appreciation of creativity and Capra's creativity) that we can either diffuse (limitations) or use (talents) what we've got.

To accept ourselves, we must know ourselves. Interestingly, if we accept the idea that we'll accept *whatever* we discover about ourselves, it makes the knowing easier. When we no longer struggle with the fear of what *might be,* and accept that we'll accept *whatever* we find out, then self-discovery can be a journey of fascination and curiosity, not one of foreboding, denial, and dread.

*The last quarter of a century
of my life has been
pretty constantly
and faithfully devoted
to the study of the human race—
that is to say,
the study of myself,
for in my individual person
I am the entire human race
compacted together.*

*I have found that
there is no ingredient
of the race
which I do not possess
in either a small way
or a large way.*

MARK TWAIN

Self-Knowledge

What can be more fundamental than the ancient admonition "know thyself"? Shakespeare's "To thine own self be true" may be well and good, but if we don't know what our own self is, how can we be true to it?

We need to take a straight-ahead, lights-on, ruthless, flattering, unflinching look at ourselves and say, "That's me!" Twelve-step programs recommend "taking a searching and fearless moral inventory." Self-knowledge tends to be less a process of discovery than of *acknowledgment*—another word for *acceptance*. For the most part, we already know ourselves—we've just been spending a lot of time refusing to admit (or actively hiding) what we already know to be true.

The stuff we *suspect* in the deep, dark reaches of our awareness—that's probably true. The greatness we perceive only in our most grandiose daydreams—that's probably true, too. Again, knowing that we don't have to *do* anything about this information—even judge it—makes it easier to acknowledge.

For most people, accepting exceptional aspects of themselves is far more difficult than acknowledging nasty ones. Thanks to parents, teachers, and other authority figures, we've been taught to "break down" and accept the negative criticism. Seldom does an authority figure "break through" our barriers in order to tell us how *good* a given aspect of ourselves is. When exploring the part of ourselves

> *It's not only the most difficult thing
> to know one's self,
> but the most inconvenient.*
>
> JOSH BILLINGS

we have not yet acknowledged, then, we tend to look for the dark stuff.

Keeping this in mind as you make your exploration of self, it might be a good idea to find a positive attribute for every limitation you find.

This can be difficult because we have also been trained to take our positive qualities for granted. Taking something for granted is like putting it away in a closet and forgetting about it. Yes, we own it, we control it, and we can use it whenever we want—but if we have forgotten it's there, we won't. This is why I included the word *flattering* at the top of this chapter when describing the sort of self-evaluation to do. In your view of both the *bad* and the *good*, you may find that, like most people, you flinch more at the positive qualities—and move into a smoother, almost automatic denial of them. But go ahead. Acknowledge your good. Flinch a little.

You might want to make two lists—one labeled "Qualities" and one labeled "Limitations." As you continue exploring yourself (which will probably be an ongoing process), you can add qualities and limitations to your list. If you want to get a head start on some exercises we'll be doing later in the book, write your qualities and limitations on 3x5 cards—one quality or limitation per card.

In time, you may find certain qualities wandering from list to list. What you thought was impatience, a limitation, might be used to compensate for procrastination, thus becoming an attribute. Procrastination might be used to compensate for impulsiveness, turning procrastination into an attribute as well.

When we look outside ourselves, we tend to evaluate. These evaluations tell us about the people and things around us.

These evaluations also tell us about *ourselves*.

It's known as the *mirror concept*. The mirror concept goes like this: Whatever we find "true" about the people and things around us, is also true about ourselves. When we evaluate anything outside ourselves, what we are doing is looking into a mirror—the mirror reflects back to us information about ourselves.

You may not always *like* what you see in the mirror; you may not always be comfortable with it;

> *If people can be educated to see*
> *the lowly side of their own natures,*
> *it may be hoped that they will also learn*
> *to understand and to love*
> *their fellow men better.*
>
> *A little less hypocrisy*
> *and a little more tolerance*
> *toward oneself can only have good results*
> *in respect for our neighbor;*
> *for we are all too prone to transfer*
> *to our fellows the injustice and violence*
> *we inflict upon our own natures.*
>
> CARL JUNG

but, if you want to learn about yourself more quickly, looking at yourself in the mirror of people and things is a valuable tool.

Remember the first time you heard your voice on a tape recorder, or saw yourself on videotape? "I don't sound like that! I don't behave that way!" Meanwhile, all your friends are saying, "Yes, that's what you sound like. Yes, that's precisely how you behave."

The first time *I* saw myself on videotape, I wondered how I had any friends at all. In time, with repeated viewings, I learned to accept the images of myself on the tape, and from that point of acceptance, I could begin making changes. (I like to think of them as *improvements.*)

And so it is with the mirror of life. You may not like all you see in the mirror, but until you look into the mirror and accept all that you see *about yourself*, you will not be able to make the changes, compensations, or improvements you'd like.

Let's say you look at someone and think, "She is angry, and I don't like that." Could it be you don't like being angry? If you observe someone and say, "He's afraid to act. I wish he'd just *do it*." Could there be something you're afraid of; something you wish you would "just do"?

Sometimes, we have to shift our focus a bit to see what it is about ourselves that's being reflected by others. For example, you may look at someone smoking and not like it. You might say, "I don't smoke, how does that apply to me?"

What is it you don't like about the other person's smoking? "It's unhealthy." What do you do that's not healthy? "Smoking is inconsiderate." What do you do that's inconsiderate? "Smoking is a bad habit." What's your worst habit? "It's a waste of money." How do you waste money? "It shows a lack of self-control." Where could you use more self-control?

Get the idea? There are other people's actions, and then there are the judgments we place on those actions. If we move from the *action* we judge, and look at the *judgment*, we usually find a similar judgment we make about ourselves.

It's fun to extend this idea beyond people and include things: "This car never works when I want it to." What about you never works when you want it to? "It always rains at the worst possible time." What do you do at the worst possible time? "This steak is

> *I just look in the mirror*
> *and I say*
> *"God, it's really fantastic,*
> *the Lord really gave me something."*
>
> *So why on earth*
> *should I cover any of it up.*
>
> EDY WILLIAMS

too tough." What about you could use tenderizing?

The mirror gives you lots of material on which to practice acceptance. You can learn to accept everything you already know about yourself, as well as everything you learn by looking into the mirror of other people's behavior. Your harshest judgments of others are the very ones that will benefit you most if you accept them about yourself.

The mirror also focuses you back on something (that is, *someone*) you *can* do something about. (Ever notice how little effect your judgments have on others?) All that good advice you've been giving to others (or would gladly give them if they only had the wisdom to ask) *finally* has a home. You.

And, as you're the only one you can really

change, the only one who can really use all your good advice is you. Like other aspects of self-love, the *advice giver* and the *best user* of the advice are the same person.

When we look into the mirror of life and see all there is within ourselves that needs improvement, we know we're going to be at it for some time: changing what we can, doing our best with what we can't, accepting and forgiving it all.

We also see that whenever we lash out at another, we are really lashing out at ourselves. In this context, to strike another is as silly as striking the bathroom mirror because it's giving us a reflection we don't like. We can only pray that in our striking out, we don't hurt the mirror (especially when that mirror is another person). Could that be where the superstition, "If you break a mirror, it's seven years bad luck," comes from?

Thus far, I've only been talking about the "glass darkly" side of the mirror concept. It does have a lighter side—mirrors also reflect what's good about us.

All the people and things you find loving, affectionate, caring, devoted, tender, wonderful, compassionate, beautiful, adorable, magnificent, and sacred are simply mirroring to you the loving, affectionate, caring, devoted, tender, wonderful, compassionate, beautiful, adorable, magnificent, and sacred aspects of yourself.

"When I see the majesty of a mountain, what does that have to do with me?" Everything. That purple mountain majesty is in you, too. In fact, it's not really in the mountain *at all*. What's in the

> *Resolve to be thyself:*
> *and know, that he*
> *Who finds himself,*
> *loses his misery.*

MATTHEW ARNOLD

mountain is *rock*. What we, as humans, *project onto* the mountain is majesty.

That's one of the reasons the mirror concept works. Most of the time we are projecting *something* onto almost *everything.* When the projection returns to us, we can see it as a reflection—which it is—or we can pretend it is emanating from whatever or whomever we projected the reflection onto.

The illusion that what we projected is coming from the thing we projected it onto is deceptive. We tend to get lost in the illusion, just as we tend to get lost in the illusion of images projected on a movie screen. It is, nonetheless, an illusion, and the source of the projection at the movie theater is the projector. The source of what we think and feel about others is ourselves.

Using the mirror concept, we can begin to recognize the true source of the projections we make. We begin to see that this person wasn't so bad after all. It was, in fact, what we were projecting onto him. We see that this other person wasn't so wonderful after all. We were merely projecting our wonderfulness upon her.

The more you use it, the more you will probably find the mirror concept works. It doesn't work in every case, of course—some people *are* rat bastards—but it works often enough to prove a useful tool for expanding self-knowledge.

Eventually, we see there really is no right or wrong about us, any more than a symphony orchestra has right or wrong instruments. Each instrument has its place and its player. The goal is to orchestrate and conduct the spectacular range of abilities, behaviors, desires, reactions, actions, and inactions that is uniquely *you* into a harmonic whole.

How? The book is far from over. In fact, I seem to hear the familiar strains of an orchestra tuning up.

If you have
anything really valuable
to contribute
to the world
it will come through
the expression
of your own personality,
that single spark of divinity
that sets you off
and makes you different
from every other
living creature.

BRUCE BARTON

Self-Worth

Worthiness is often a misunderstood idea. People seem to believe they need to *work hard* in order to become worthy. This is not true. In fact, you don't have to work at all to be worthy of whatever you have or are.*

The obvious fact is—if you are not worthy, you wouldn't have it. Whatever you've got, you're worthy of. Legitimate** possession proves worthiness. Lack of possession indicates a lack of worthiness.

Nowhere is this concept more true than in the idea of *self*-worth.

How can we *not* be worthy of what we already *are?* How can we not be worthy of the attributes we already have? Of course we are worthy of ourselves, and all that ourselves entail.

Then why don't we *feel* worthy? Because how we *feel* about ourselves—how we rate our attributes and limitations on that ever-present, internal scale of one-to-ten—is how we *esteem* ourselves.

---

*If you want *more*, however, that probably will take work.

**By *legitimate* I mean that if you stole something, you might not feel worthy of it—and you would be right.

*You have no idea what
a poor opinion
I have of myself—
and how little I deserve it.*

W. S. GILBERT

Self-Esteem

Thus far in our journey toward loving ourselves, we have gotten to know ourselves a little better, accepted what we discovered, and even accepted that we are worthy of what we are. Now, let's start *liking* ourselves a little better.

How we view ourselves—*esteem* ourselves—is central to self-love. Why would we want to take care of, with regular intervals of taking *good* care of, and occasionally splurge on pampering someone we didn't hold in good esteem?

For the most part, we don't have to do or be any better than we are to feel better about ourselves. You simply have to *remember* the good that you are and the good that you've done.

As I previously mentioned, most of us take our good for granted while we shine brighter and brighter searchlights on our bad. In addition to whatever genetic predisposition toward personal pessimism we have, our upbringing only added to it. When you learned how to tie your shoe, you got praise. Each successive time you tied your shoe, the praise was less. Soon, tying your shoe was taken for granted—it was expected. Then when you failed to tie your shoe, it was met with disapproval. The more often you didn't tie your shoe, the more the disapproval grew. The good (tying the shoe) was given less attention while the bad (not tying the shoe) was given more.

By the time we got to school (which should be called expectation school and not elementary

> *I have little patience with anyone*
> *who is not self-satisfied.*
>
> *I am always pleased to see my friends,*
> *happy to be with my wife and family,*
> *but the high spot of every day*
> *is when I first catch a glimpse*
> *of myself in the shaving mirror.*

ROBERT MORLEY

school), as soon as we learned one thing (the A's), it was taken for granted and we went right on to something even more intricate (the B's). Soon the entire alphabet was taken for granted and we were expected to print any letter on demand. Then came *cursive* writing. Curses. Words. Sentences. *Spelling!* It never stopped. Science, history, geography; grade after grade, year after year. I'm getting exhausted just thinking about it.

This is, for the most part, what we do to ourselves. If we are naturally generous and enjoy giving to others, we see our giving as a given. If we, from time to time, feel fearful about something we "know" there is no need to feel fearful about, we see the bout with anxiety not as a new battle, but yet another skirmish in the ongoing saga or our own "inability to conquer fear." Our generosity, which in the overall scheme of things does much more good than the fearful episodes do harm, is not in our awareness given the proper weight. We remember the fear and forget the giving. Thus our self-esteem is low.

The solution, obviously, is to remember more of the good. Stop taking the good that you are and do for granted.

Stop.

For this, writing your own "Good Book," can be invaluable. Get a blank book of any kind (or open a new computer file) and list all the good things you do each day. It doesn't need to be an essay, just a few words to memorialize each good deed. (Or, if you're breaking a bad habit, the lack of a negative deed: "Smoked two fewer cigarettes today.") Focus especially on the good you take for granted.

In time, the book fills with the accomplishments we otherwise tend to forget. By rereading the list, we remind ourselves of the good that we do and the good that we are. We begin to feel better about the person who accomplishes so much goodness—ourselves. Our self-esteem is enhanced.

We can also enhance our self-esteem through self-talk. We talk to ourselves all the time anyway; we might as well use that time to convince ourselves of what is already true—that we are a pretty neat person. When you do something good, rather than just letting it pass, give yourself a little praise. No. Give yourself *a lot* of praise. Let the praise last until the next good thing you do. Then praise that.

> *Twenty-four years ago*
> *I was strangely handsome;*
> *in San Francisco*
> *in the rainy season*
> *I was often mistaken for fair weather.*

MARK TWAIN

When we start looking for the good to praise rather than the bad to condemn, we tend to find the good. Most people discover it's amazing just how much good they actually do—without increasing the amount of good they do. Of course, increasing the amount of good helps, too. But most people make the mistake of increasing the good they do, and not remembering the new good any more than they remember the old good.

If you don't remember your goodness, it is not going to help your self-esteem at all. In fact, not giving yourself credit sometimes has the reverse effect—the more good you do, the more you expect from yourself, which only leads to the twin devils of exhaustion (if you live up to the expectation) and disappointment (if you don't).

As we praise ourselves in our self-talk for the good we do, and remember the good that we do by writing in and reviewing our Good Book, we think better of ourselves, our self-esteem rises, and we tend to have more self-confidence.

He who hesitates
is a damned fool.

MAE WEST

Self-Confidence

The poster woman of self-confidence must surely be Mae West. In 1932, she arrived in a Hollywood that worshiped youth and skinniness—a holdover of the flappers from the Roaring '20s. Mae, who had considerable success in Vaudeville and on the Broadway stage, was forty and buxom. By the Hollywood standards of the day, she would almost certainly have been relegated to "character parts," playing the mother of the picture's star, but never the star herself.

When she got off the train in Los Angeles, she told the assembled reporters (whom she had personally assembled): "I'm not a little girl from a little town making good in a big town. I'm a big girl from a big town making good in a little town." In 1934, she made more money than anyone in the United States, other than William Randolph Hearst. She single-handedly redefined what Americans considered sexy. In a film career that spanned nearly fifty years, she never played a mother.

While our self-confidence need not be as flamboyant as Mae West's, it can be just as effective.

Self-confidence is simply knowing that you can do whatever is most important to you. Those who say you can't aren't necessarily against you—they just haven't caught on yet. Their learning curve concerning your abilities is more gradual than your own.

No, we can't do everything we want or be everything we'd like to be, but we can feel confident about

> *Calm self-confidence*
> *is as far from conceit*
> *as the desire*
> *to earn a decent living*
> *is remote from greed.*
>
> CHANNING POLLOCK

what we know we can do, and about what we already are.

If, for example, I said, "I'm going to write a chapter tomorrow," that would be confidence. If, on the other hand, I said, "I'm going to run a marathon tomorrow," that wouldn't be confidence—that would be pure con. For me. For a practiced marathon runner, the opposite might be true.

Where do we draw the line between self-confidence and self-conning? Make your goals and views of self realistic—but leave ample room for growth.

Most of us do just the opposite. We take the irrefutable evidence of past successes and whittle it down into an acceptable, overly modest self-view.

That whittling can be significant, too—some turn telephone poles into toothpicks.

Self-confidence is primarily demonstrated by doing. We seldom think, "Oh, I have enough self-confidence to . . ." about what we are truly self-confident. You are confident, for example, about reading English. Before plowing into this sentence, you probably didn't have to think, "I am confident that I can read this sentence." Nor did I contemplate my ability to write the sentence. We just did it. (And I must say we did a *marvelous* job, didn't we?)

Here, again, your Good Book comes in handy. The things you have done often in the past you can be fairly certain of doing again. That's self-confidence. Like self-esteem, you simply need to remember you did them.

Self-confidence also includes being confident about who we are. Self-confidence is knowing that we are what we are and we don't have to apologize to anyone for it. Nor do we have to indulge (and exhaust) ourselves in the pre-apologetic behaviors of concealing, denying, and pretending.

Self-confidence is being able to say to another, "I am what I am, and as long as I am not physically harming you or your property, your not liking what I am is *your* problem." It can be said without malice. In fact, you can even say it in such a way (try imitating Mae West, for example) that the recipient of your self-confidence will smile and accept you for who you are.

*The important thing
is not to stop questioning.*

*Curiosity has its own reason
for existing.*

*One cannot help but be in awe
when he contemplates
the mysteries of eternity, of life,
of the marvelous structure of reality.*

*It is enough if one tries
merely to comprehend
a little of this mystery every day.*

Never lose a holy curiosity.

ALBERT EINSTEIN

Self-Service

No, this is not the chapter on masturbation. That comes later. This is a chapter about doing all those things for yourself that you don't want to do, but you'd be a lot happier if you got them done.

Generally, the term *service* refers to doing good for others whether we feel like doing it in that moment or not. We volunteer to answer the phone for our favorite charity, for example. When the appointed phone-answering hour arrives, we go down and answer the phone even if what we *feel* like doing in that moment is watching TV. With friends, this is called doing them a favor. With family and country (those inseparable concepts), it's known as doing your duty.

We serve country, family, friends, and even strangers—so why not serve ourselves as well? As we look around, we probably see any number of things that need doing. From straightening up (or shoveling out) the living room to putting the CDs in alphabetical order (after putting them back in their little plastic cases, of course), our lives are probably cluttered with things that "we'd be a lot better off" if we would only "take care of them."

Self-service is taking care of them.

It's a matter of keeping the agreements that you make with yourself just as you would keep agreements with significant others. Would you keep an agreement with your best friend? Your doctor? Your mother? Your parole officer? Then keep it with yourself.

> *Humility is not my forte,*
> *and whenever I dwell*
> *for any length of time*
> *on my own shortcomings,*
> *they gradually begin to seem*
> *mild, harmless,*
> *rather engaging little things.*
>
> MARGARET HALSEY

There's no need to be harsh with yourself—you are, after all, doing it with, and for, the love of your life (you). But, no matter how many self-help books I read (or write) about the importance of "being in the moment," some things just aren't worth being in the moment with. Don't even attempt to enjoy such activities—just get them done (or get rich enough to hire someone else to do them); then enjoy the fact that they *are* done. That's the satisfaction of self-service.

At other times, self-service means invoking self-acceptance. When it comes to cleaning our house or apartment, we can take comfort from Quentin Crisp, who claims that he did not clean his apartment in London for more than twenty-five years: "After the first four years, it doesn't get any dirtier," he said. "It's just a question of not losing your *nerve*." No matter how unlike the Cleaver household our domicile appears, the chances are it doesn't look like Quentin Crisp's. We can take comfort in that.

A fundamental question we must ask ourselves is: "Does this need doing?" Before answering that question, perhaps you should hand-letter a sign and place it on the wall of every room in your house:

ACCEPTANCE IS A LOT LESS WORK

If you choose to accept rather than do, then *really* accept it. Don't look at the pile of dirty laundry each time you pass by it (or over it, or through it) and berate yourself for not having done the laundry. Remember that you *accepted* the laundry in its current state for a certain number of days (weeks, months, years). Here we return again to keeping agreements.

If something must eventually be done, such as the laundry, we can accept putting it off for, say, three more days, but after three days we've accepted enough and it's time to start washing clothes. If something doesn't need to get done but it would be nice if it got done eventually, accept its undoneness until eventually.

In being of service to yourself, ask yourself: If I were asked by the person I love most in this world (other than myself) to do this right now, would I do it? If the answer is yes, then do it for yourself. If someone you loved most in the world asked you to accept something about himself or herself, would you accept it? Then accept it about yourself, too.

*Murder
is always a mistake.*

*One should never
do anything
that one cannot talk about
after dinner.*

OSCAR WILDE

Self-Respect

It is hard to love anyone we don't respect, and that is especially true of ourselves. We know more about our dark side than anyone else and, if the image we have of a respectable human being is someone without a dark side, respecting ourselves can be nearly impossible.

To respect ourselves, we must (there are two ways of putting this, take your choice): (a) accept ourselves as a human being, knowing that human beings aren't perfect; or (b) lower our standards.

Rather than make a long list of all the mistakes a person worthy of self-respect might occasionally make, allow me to provide four fundamental statements I believe a person worthy of self-respect should be able to make.

1. I take care of my basic needs. It is difficult to respect ourselves if we are without food, shelter, clothing, or are not looking after the basics of physical cleanliness and disease prevention.

2. I do not physically harm the person or property of another. It's hard to respect ourselves if we go about physically harming other people or their property—unless they give their permission or the harming occurs in self-defense. This respect for others, in fact, is the basis of any society that rises above the law of the jungle (might makes right; survival of the fittest). This also means we don't cheat people or steal from them. As Woody Guthrie said, "Some people rob you with a six gun, and others rob you with a fountain pen." If self-respect is what

> *The superior man*
> *will not manifest*
> *either narrow-mindedness*
> *or the want of self-respect.*
>
> MENCIUS
> 372–289 B.C.

we seek, we don't do either.

3. I avoid truly stupid risks with my own person and property. Before you do something that *physically* endangers you or your property, ask yourself: "If this goes wrong, will I shake my head and say, 'Boy, what a dumb thing to have done.'" If so, don't do it. If, on the other hand, you would say after even the worst-case scenario, "Well, that's the breaks of the game," go ahead and do it. It's impossible to make life risk free, and people who take no risks whatsoever can have a lot of trouble respecting themselves. At the other end of the spectrum, there are risks we know are stupid when we are doing them, and we still know they're stupid even when we get away with them. The term in law when you do this to someone else is *reckless endangerment*. Don't recklessly endanger yourself, either.

4. I don't hurt other people emotionally just for the sake of hurting them. It's futile to say, "I don't hurt other people emotionally," because, in merely expressing our own preferences or following our own goals, we may emotionally hurt some people. We may not even *know* these people. I've gotten letters from people who were *so hurt* by something I wrote in a book or said in an interview that (according to them) I should be *ashamed* of myself. (You can image how many people will be *so hurt* by my view of romantic love.) My intention was not to emotionally upset them, but simply to state my honest point of view as accurately as possible; they felt hurt nonetheless.

In stating our personal, religious, or political opinions, we run the risk of hurting others. In fact, if our opinions become circulated widely enough, it is almost guaranteed that a certain percentage of people will be in emotional upheaval (in some circles known as *high dungeon*) due to our statements. It is not our statements at all, of course, that upset these people, but their beliefs *about* our statement. The only thing to say about those situations is, "Too bad."

The same is true in the more delicate areas of personal relationships, in which people we know—people we care about—feel hurt because we tell them we're moving, changing jobs, gay, not going to Cousin Sadie's wedding, or in some other way not doing it the way they want it done. Although "too bad" is too harsh a response for people we care

> *Character—*
> *the willingness*
> *to accept responsibility*
> *for one's own life—*
> *is the source from which*
> *self-respect springs.*
>
> JOAN DIDION

about, we cannot in good conscience allow their emotional upheaval to dictate our behavior—at least not *too* often.

The emotionally-hurting-others-for-hurt's-sake I'm suggesting you avoid is what we tend to do when we are, say, arguing with someone we love and we "drop the bomb." In an effort to annihilate rather than illuminate, we slip in the zinger (which is more hurtful than true) or exaggerate the facts (read: *lie*) in order to win (knowing that the other person's loss will be hurtful).

Similarly, if we unnecessarily play "take away" to punish the people we care about for their "bad behavior," or if we stay emotionally or physically distant longer than necessary, we could be guilty of trying to make *them* feel guilty and of doing it not just intentionally, but *gleefully*. If you want to retain your self-respect (and your relationships), don't do this *too* often, either.

To my four suggested rules for self-respect, you might want to add your own list of actions "no self-respecting person would do." But please don't get carried away. Make this the *fundamental* list of violations, not every *faux pas*, breach of manners, or error in etiquette human beings are heir to. There's quite a difference between not being polite and outright cruelty. Deny yourself self-respect only for activities at the cruel end of the spectrum.

You may have noticed that a lot about self-respect comes down to *intention*. When we make a mistake, we may mess up a great deal and still keep our self-respect. Our intention was not to hurt, but an honest error caused harm. Conversely, if we intend harm, and relatively little damage is done, that intention to harm can shoot a fairly large hole in the respect we have for ourselves.

When dealing with self-respect, stick to the basics. As we discussed, self-esteem has to do with thinking well of yourself and liking yourself. For now, just take a look at respect. We can often respect people we don't like—a worthy opponent, a controversial figure, even a politician. (As Henry Kissinger said, "Ninety percent of the politicians give the rest of us a bad name.")

I would be willing to bet a reasonable sum of money (not a stupidly exorbitant amount) that you

> *Some persons are likeable*
> *in spite of their*
> *unswerving integrity.*
>
> DON MARQUIS

already are, and have been, behaving in a way that warrants your self-respect—and a good deal more.

Adultery is a meanness and a stealing, a taking away from someone what should be theirs, a great selfishness, and surrounded and guarded by lies lest it should be found out.

And out of meanness and selfishness and lying flow love and joy and peace beyond anything that can be imagined.

DAME ROSE MACAULAY

A Code of Honor: Never approach a friend's girlfriend or wife with mischief as your goal.

There are just too many women in the world to justify that sort of dishonorable behavior.

Unless she's <u>really</u> attractive.

BRUCE JAY FRIEDMAN

*Self criticism
must be
my guide to action,
and the first rule
for its employment
is that in itself
it is not a virtue,
only a procedure.*

KINGSLEY AMIS

Self-Criticism

If all you did was languish about, accepting and praising everything about yourself, you would eventually slip into complacency, and a complacent lover is hardly a lover at all. It might even be stated that complacency is the very antithesis of love.

When I think of complacency, I remember a film of an unfortunate amoeba we were shown in elementary school. First they showed an amoeba (not the unfortunate one, but another one) that had such a hostile environment, it died. (How they got away with showing amoeba snuff films to sixth graders I'll never know.)

Then they showed an amoeba that had a moderately nurturing environment, but was nevertheless challenged by an amoeba's version of occasional slings and arrows of outrageous fortune. This caused the amoeba to move, do, and grow. This amoeba thrived, and headed directly to the local Kinko's where it reproduced itself many times over.

Then we came to the unfortunate amoeba. The unfortunate amoeba was placed in the ideal environment, a sort of amoeboid Nirvana. This amoeba was never challenged at all. It grew larger and larger and larger until it simply *came apart*.

The outer environment was *so* ideal that the amoeba must have thought, "Why waste all this energy keeping up a cell wall?" The amoeba seemed to dissolve into its surroundings.

Another example of complacency is that of lying in a hot bath. If you lie perfectly still in water

> *I can take any amount of criticism,*
> *so long as it is unqualified praise.*
>
> NOEL COWARD

that is just hot enough but not too hot, it is hard to feel where your body ends the water begins. In fact, after you lie motionless for a while in this "just right" environment, sensation itself seems to disappear—you begin to lose track of your body altogether. How do you feel your body and the hot water again? *You make waves.*

That's what self-criticism is—making waves. Self-criticism is a spur to action, achievement, and growth; a guarantee against complacency.

The problem with self-criticism is that almost all of us take it too far—*everything* we are and do is up for critical grabs. We compare everything about ourselves to an imaginary ideal, and of course we fall short again and again. This sort of criticism is withering. It inspires rebellion, confusion, pain, and numbness—not growth.

Far from urging one to act, it discourages one from any action at all. It is oppressive, not stimulating; contractive, not expansive.

Self-criticism in the context of self-love, on the other hand, selects very carefully the areas in which criticism is permitted. It only delivers the criticism that will help us get to our goals, to achieve what we really want. It is, as they say, *constructive criticism*.

As we shall explore later in this book, it is important for us to select carefully what we want to accomplish. Like a lengthy menu in a large restaurant, the list of our desires is far greater than the time we have to obtain and enjoy them all. From the menu we can choose *anything* we want to eat, but we can't eat *everything*—there's just not enough room to put it, not enough time to wait around for more room to become available, and perhaps not enough money to pay for it all. We must, then, choose carefully what we want to pursue, and let the rest of the goals go by.

All the goals we are not pursuing are not acceptable subjects for self-criticism. If we have decided that "losing weight" is not a high priority, we do not get to think, "tsk, tsk, tsk" every time we look in a mirror (or look down). ("Hey! Hey! Hey!" is okay.) If we have chosen not to fight the battle of the bulge (which is genetic and takes a great deal of time and effort to fight), we, as self-lovers, are not entitled to criticize our bulge. Unless the excess weight is *truly* endangering our health in a *major* way, this is a category for self-acceptance, not self-criticism.

> *Criticism,*
> *as it was*
> *first instituted by Aristotle,*
> *was meant*
> *as a standard of judging well.*
>
> DR. SAMUEL JOHNSON

Say, on the other hand, we choose to do three thirty-minute sessions of aerobic exercise per week in order to keep our cardiovascular system from looking like the clogged pipe in those Drano ads. When our moment on the torture rack—I mean, happy half-hour on the exercise bicycle—approaches, self-criticism can be invaluable when we turn it loose on the brilliant objections, excuses, and rationalizations we have concocted since our last unwilling—that is, joyous—visit to Perspiration Row.

What self-criticism has in its favor is *your choice*. You *chose* to make aerobics more important than excuses, and it's self-criticism's job to make sure the unwilling portions of you (which, when being uncooperative, are *not* in alignment with self-love) don't "win."

Seldom does it need to be a battle. Generally, self-criticism consists of steady reminders with occasional negotiation sessions.

It's also self-criticism's job to praise when the dirty deed is done. We seem to automatically associate the word *criticism* with negative evaluation. This is not the case. Criticism also praises the good. And that's what self-criticism does most of the time—if we would only listen.

Self-criticism doesn't just shoot arrows when we are errant in our ways—when we do something good, it sends bouquets. Far from the exclusively acid-tongued tyrant many of us think (and have experienced) self-criticism to be, self-criticism can laud just as well as it can lay low.

Naturally, if we go considerably off our path, self-criticism has a sting. If it didn't, what would keep complacency from taking over? The message from self-criticism at these times is not, "You *must* do this *now*," but, "If you don't want the goal that makes this action necessary, just let me know and I'll take the goal off your list."

Certainly, self-criticism stings harshest when we contemplate harming the person or property of another, or doing something that has a high likelihood of harming ourselves. And this is as it should be.

For most people, however, and certainly for almost everyone reading this book, self-love will mean turning down the floodlight that shines so brightly on "anything that is wrong," and focusing a precise beam on the specific areas we choose to improve.

*Good habits, which bring
our lower passions and appetites
under automatic control,
leave our natures free to explore
the larger experiences of life.*

*Too many of us
divide and dissipate our energies
in debating actions
which should be taken for granted.*

Ralph W. Sockman

Self-Discipline

Working hand in hand with self-criticism is self-discipline. Discipline usually implies punishment exacted by a harsh authoritarian figure. It brings to mind images from old movies of a bald general wearing a monocle, sneering in a thick foreign accent, "If you do not behave, ve vill have to *discipline you!*"

Allow me to put those images to rest. You will not have to shave your head, wear a monocle, or learn a foreign accent in order to apply self-discipline. In fact, you already apply self-discipline in thousands of ways you don't even think of. That's the purpose of self-discipline: to form a good habit.

Take reading, for example—something I assume most of you are doing right now. (I have no idea what the rest of you are doing.*) When we first learned to read, every word was a struggle. Putting the meaning of a sentence together was a time-consuming, demanding chore. Today, book in one hand, apple in the other, we don't even "think" about reading. We just read. It's a habit. A good habit.

The same is true of speaking, walking, chewing with our mouths closed, making a phone call, and so many other activities. To develop a good habit requires a lot of self-discipline (practice, practice, practice), and to maintain the habit requires a much smaller, but still measurable, amount of self-discipline. In reading, for example, maintenance

---

*But I hope you are having a good time, whatever it is.

> *Cultivate only the habits*
> *that you are willing*
> *should master you.*
>
> ELBERT HUBBARD

may mean looking up all of the preternatural words. This keeps our vocabulary puissant. Although brushing our teeth is nearly automatic now, going to the sink and pulling out the toothbrush may take a tad of self-discipline.

Discipline comes from the word *disciple*—to be a loving student of. Self-discipline is being a loving student of—you guessed it—*yourself.*

If you notice, for example, that you spend an inordinate amount of time looking for your keys, some part of you (the self-disciplinarian, perhaps) says, "You know, if we would put our keys in the same place each time we got home, they would be in that place the next time we needed them." If we deem that not only a good idea, but an idea worth implementing, self-discipline (and its dear companion self-criticism) will begin the process of consciously reminding us to put the keys in the same place, so that eventually we will unconsciously (automatically) put the keys in that place almost every time.

Many people think of self-discipline as what is required to break a bad habit. Why not, instead, see it as a way of making a new, good habit? Then self-discipline doesn't have to be associated with *breaking* anything.

Let's say you consider smoking a bad habit and you want to eliminate it. Rather than breaking the bad habit of smoking, why not think of your self-discipline as creating a new habit of not smoking? How do you create the habit of not smoking? Whenever you want to smoke, do something else. *Anything* else. Eventually (and I'm not for a moment pretending it's not a lot of work), you will be in the habit of not smoking, just as you're currently in the habit of not getting a tattoo every Saturday night, not flushing dollar bills down the toilet, and not leaning over incinerators and inhaling deeply. (If, however, you smoke and have decided not to try to stop, accept it. There is no point in adding self-judgment and guilt to whatever harm the cigarettes are doing.)

Self-discipline is a powerful tool for creating and maintaining good habits. Good habits let us love ourselves—automatically.

*The spirit of self-help
is the root of all genuine growth
in the individual; and,
exhibited in the lives of many,
it constitutes the true source
of national vigor and strength.*

*Help from without
is often enfeebling in its effects,
but help from within
invariably invigorates.*

SAMUEL SMILES
1859

Self-Improvement

I don't like the term *self-improvement*. It seems to imply that there is something to improve—that we are not just fine the way we are. I prefer the term *personal growth*. Growth implies a natural progression from one perfectly spectacular state to another. A tree may be great now, and in a year will have grown into even more greatness. A puppy grows into a dog or a kitten grows into a cat without being anything less than ideal all along the way.

That, I think, is how we should view ourselves. There is no "perfect us" that we will reach "out there" in the future, at which time we will be whole. We're whole now. We're the whole of all that we are. Yes, we're wholly. Wholly us.

When we simply nurture ourselves, personal growth takes place effortlessly—without any planning on our part. If we feed ourselves some uplifting ideas; give ourselves room to make mistakes; forgive ourselves; accept ourselves; and (of course) take care of ourselves, with regular intervals of taking *good* care of ourselves, and occasional splurges of pampering; we'll grow—naturally, beautifully, splendidly.

Like a tree, we don't have to say, "I think a branch should come out here, and on these points leaves should appear." We water the tree, give it some fertilizer, and watch nature work its magic.

Isn't life the most incredible, delightful, wondrous, awe-inspiring mystery? I love to watch nature documentaries; they never lose the power to astound me. Watching the wondrous dance of plants

> *Self-reverence,*
> *self-knowledge,*
> *self-control,*
> *These three alone*
> *lead life to*
> *sovereign power.*
>
> ALFRED, LORD TENNYSON

and animals makes me utter one involuntary, "God!" after another, as I marvel at the mystery of life, with its precision, creativity, and boundless enthusiasm. I have given up trying to figure out the mystery. I'm working on relaxing and letting myself simply enjoy it.

So, too, are we a part of that dance; but our steps are more intricate, our abilities more magnificent, and our power more awe-full.

We need not decide every detail and direction our growth will take. We need but nurture ourselves and enjoy the mystery of creation.

Humans are unique, however, in that we can nudge our growth in certain directions. What is the best way of doing that? By paying for it. The more we spend of two of our more precious resources, the more we tend to grow in the direction we spend them on.

These resources are *time* and *attention*. If we want to move in a certain area, the more time we spend reading about, talking about, exploring, practicing, imagining, affirming, and doing it, the more quickly we grow in that direction.

In addition to growth, nurturing ourselves has a way of quietly encouraging *quality*. I'm assuming you just don't just want to *grow*, but you want your growth to represent a greater excellence.

Oscar Wilde explained the importance of time in producing quality. He said he labored all morning on a poem, and by the end of the morning had removed but a single comma. He went to lunch, and returned to his poem and spent the remainder of the afternoon on it. He put the comma back in.

That might seem like the waste of a day, but not to Wilde. In his quest for quality, he would never have to question that comma again.

That's how personal growth seems to go. We spend a lot of time and attention on something only to return precisely to the point we started. But at least we know that the point at which we started is where we want to be. At least for now.

As you begin to blossom, it may turn out that you are a lime tree and not a lemon tree. Not bad at all—just make Margaritas instead of lemonade. You may sit down intent on writing a self-help book, and wind up with a sitcom. (I've been accused of this, even though I'm *still* publishing this as a self-help book.) You may set out to be a great dancer and

> *Is life so wretched?*
>
> *Isn't it rather your hands*
> *which are too small,*
> *your vision which is muddied.*
>
> *You are the one who must grow up.*
>
> DAG HAMMARSKJÖLD

find that you prefer teaching others to dance.

In nurturing yourself, you discover more and more of your personal nature.

Let it grow, let it grow, let it grow.

*Some of us are becoming the men
we wanted to marry.*

GLORIA STEINEM

*Love is an act
of endless forgiveness.*

PETER USTINOV

Self-Forgiveness

Forgiving means "for giving"—*in favor of* giving.

When you forgive another, to whom do you give? The other? Sometimes. Yourself? *Always.* To forgive another is being in favor of giving to yourself.

In addition, most of us judge ourselves more harshly and more often than we judge others. It's important to forgive ourselves for everything we hold against ourselves.

And there is another judgment to forgive: the fact that we judged in the first place. When we judge, we leave our happiness and self-love behind—sometimes *way* behind. On some level we know this, and we judge ourselves for having judged.

The layers of forgiveness, then, are: first, the person we judged (ourselves or another); and, second, ourselves for having judged in the first place.

The technique? Simple.

Say to yourself, "I forgive _____ (NAME OF THE PERSON, PLACE, OR THING YOU JUDGED, INCLUDING YOURSELF) for _____ (THE 'TRANSGRESSION'). I forgive myself for judging _____ (SAME PERSON, PLACE, OR THING, INCLUDING YOURSELF) for _____ (WHAT YOU JUDGED)."

That's it. Simple, but amazingly effective.

If you have a lot to forgive one person for (such as yourself), you might want to invite that person into your sanctuary and forgive the person there. Yes, you can invite yourself in through your people

> *The weak can never forgive.*
>
> *Forgiveness is the attribute*
> *of the strong.*
>
> Mahatma Gandhi

mover, or you can use a mirror. Don't forget there's a FORGIVENESS ability suit in your ability suit closet. Ask your Master Teacher to join in, if you like.

That's all there is to forgiveness. Simple but powerful. How powerful? Try it for five minutes. See what happens.

After you've forgiven the transgression and the judgment, there's only one thing left to do: forget it. Whatever "protection" you think you may gain from remembering all your past grievances is far less important than the balm of forgetting.

What's the value in forgetting? It's all in the

word: *for getting*—to be in favor of getting, of receiving.

We sometimes think that shaking a fist (threateningly, with all the remembered transgressions) is the way to get something. A shaking fist tends to beget a shaking (or swinging) fist.

To receive, forgive. To get, forget.

As Henry Ward Beecher wrote:

> "I can forgive, but I cannot forget," is only another way of saying, "I will not forgive." Forgiveness ought to be like a cancelled note—torn in two, and burned up, so that it never can be shown against one.

Remembering a grievance locks you into remembering hurt, pain, anger, betrayal, and disappointment. Who on earth wants *that?* Let it go. *For give* it away. Then *for get* something new and better (light-er) in its place.

Forgive the past. Then forget it. Let it go. It is not worth remembering. None of it's worth remembering. What's worth *experiencing* is the joy of this moment.

It is easy in the world
to live after the world's opinion;
it is easy in solitude
to live after our own;
but the great man is he
who in the midst of the crowd keeps
with perfect sweetness
the independence of solitude.

RALPH WALDO EMERSON
"SELF RELIANCE"
1841

Self-Reliance

It is, of course, impossible to be completely self-reliant. We live an interdependent existence, each of us relying on mostly unseen others to fulfill our needs, while our work supports people we will never meet.

Think of all the organizations you rely on for your basic needs—the electric company, the water company, the cable company. Think of the thousands of people who work to put food on your table, clothes on your back, and a dial tone on the telephone. When you pay the bills for these services, a portion of that money goes to these people, who use it to buy *their* necessities and luxuries.

The self-reliance I am discussing, then, is not the kind that requires you to grow your own food, weave your own clothes, or (heaven forbid!) write your own books. I am speaking of a self-reliance that rejects the current cultural myth that *specific* other people are *absolutely necessary* to fulfill our emotional needs.

Many of us have been convinced that we are *emotionally unable* to do for ourselves.

Here, we return to the romantic illusion (or, perhaps more accurately, the romantic *delusion)* that if you're not loved by one significant other who is the one you love too, life is somehow incomplete.

This is simply not true.

First, any number of people who have such a relationship still feel unsatisfied—or even miserable—due to some other lack in their life: ill health, a ma-

> *Be thine own palace,*
> *or the world's thy jail.*
>
> JOHN DONNE

jor loss outside the relationship, an unfulfilled career goal, a financial setback, or so many others. An I-love-you-you-love-me-too relationship is not the panacea for all of life's ills.

Second, some people who do not have such a relationship are perfectly content with their lot. Not only is a romantic relationship not missed, it is not desired. For some, in fact, the whole notion seems silly, juvenile—something that was fun when they were young, but would have no place in their current lives.

If some people have romantic relationships and are not content while other people do not have romantic relationships and are content, romantic love must not be as much of a *need* as popular culture leads us to believe. A romance, then, might not even be that desirable a *want*. In fact, we may be able to do without a romantic relationship very well.

As with many culturally programmed desires, what makes romantic love *seem* like a need is not the lack of it, but the belief that if we had it (and it were *just right*—if it were "true love") we would be *so much* happier. What a nasty thing this cultural myth does to us. It's like someone coming up during the housewarming of our first humble apartment (one that thrills us) and telling us how much happier we would be in a five-bedroom mansion with a swimming pool, guest rooms for all our friends, a staff of servants, and a hot tub. Our studio apartment—which delighted us only a moment before—suddenly seems a bleak terrain. In fact, *anywhere* we live from that point on will be just digs until we obtain that mythical mansion in the sky (or at least on a mountain top).

Instead of realizing that we aren't likely to get such a mansion ever, we begin buying books about the great mansions of all times. We subscribe to *Mansion Digest*. We watch *Dynasty* reruns just to get a glimpse of the Carrington estate. This is precisely what people do when they fall in love with the notion of romantic love. They begin reading romance novels, buying romance magazines, watching movies heavy on romance, while putting together in their imaginations a more and more stately "mansion" known as My Romance.

Even on the slim chance that you do one day move into your mansion (romance) and it lives up

> *No one can build his security
> upon the nobleness of another person.*
>
> WILLA CATHER

to all your architectural (romantic) dreams, there is no guarantee that you'll be happy there.

I am not saying for a moment that your particular variation on the theme of romantic love (just enough time together; just the right time apart) wouldn't be *nice* to have; I am only suggesting that perhaps you don't *need* a romantic relationship to live a productive, fulfilling life. I am not against romantic love; I merely challenge the notion that, unless we are successfully living within a romantic relationship, the rest of our life is for naught.

That's just naught true.

In battle or business, whatever the game,
In law or in love, it is ever the same;
In the struggle for power,
or the scramble for pelf,
Let this be your motto—
Rely on yourself!
For, whether the prize
be a ribbon or throne,
The victor is he who can go it alone!

JOHN GODFREY SAXE
THE GAME OF LIFE

*The best things and best people
rise out of their separateness.*

*I'm against a homogenized society
because I want the cream to rise.*

ROBERT FROST

Divide and Conquer Desire

One of the nastiest myths within the myth of romantic love* is that somewhere out there is our perfect companion, lover, sex partner, friend, homemaker, mortgage payer, cook, bacon bringer, traveling companion, co–couch potato, spiritual seeker, drinking buddy, mentor, movie critic, investment expert, creative muse, financial advisor, streetwise consumer, bargain shopper, sex machine, gentle nurturer, stud muffin (or vixen), business colleague, secretary, intellectual inspirer, discussion partner, interior designer, and landscaper *all in the same person.*

Finding any *one* of these in another human being is rare and difficult enough. Finding them *all* in the *same* human being—well, what can I say? Even if you *do* find such a super-human, what are the chances that he or she will fulfill your entire relationshipal wish list *and* choose you in return?

How often have we heard the laments: "You're not the guy I fell in love with," or "You're not the same girl I met in The Gap." No, they're not; *nobody* is. The all-fulfilling lover-beloved is an *illusion.*

The only sane, logical, reasonable, sensible, and *humane* solution for both ourselves and the miserable wretches we lay our delusions upon, is to divide and conquer our desires.

If you look at the great, big, ever-hungry desire for "a lover," you'll find there is not just one desire,

*Big-time cultural myths are usually made up of myths within myths within myths, and surrounding these are dozens of auxiliary myths to keep the primary mythic labyrinth in place.

> *When it comes to women,*
> *modern men are idiots.*
>
> *They don't know what they want,*
> *and so they never want, permanently,*
> *what they get.*
>
> *They want a cream cake that*
> *is at the same time ham and eggs*
> *and at the same time porridge.*
>
> *They are fools.*
>
> *If only women weren't bound by fate*
> *to play up to them.*
>
> D. H. LAWRENCE

but dozens—perhaps hundreds—of individual desires. By dividing the Big Desire into many smaller desires, the undefined grab bag of need known as "I want to be in love" becomes subject to the rules of truth, choice, prioritization, and pursuit.

Truth. Of each of the individual desires, you can ask if you *really* want it—or, more accurately, if *you* really want it. There are certain desires that our culture assumes everybody has. Yes, perhaps the majority of people want that, but not *everybody*. Sleeping with someone every night, raising children, or having dinner each evening promptly at six, might be seen as either a dream fulfilled or a nightmare on wheels.

Choice. Some of the desires that fall within the catch-all "being in love" will fit nicely into the general direction you have chosen for your life, while some will not. What are the underlying choices—the broad strokes—you've made? Your personal Big Dream will determine, as much as anything else, which of the romantic love needs are viable for you and which are not. (More on making your big choices and selecting your major goals soon.)

Prioritization. Of the desires that do fit within your larger goals, which are the most important? Which desires, when not met for a period of time, seem to become needs? Which desires would be nice if they came waltzing along, but are not worthy of serious pursuit? Sometimes filling a single major desire fulfills a dozen smaller desires at the same time. What are your big ones?

Pursuit. Go out and get the big ones. Pursue them as you would any important goal—with a clear intention, a plan, a vision of success, an expenditure of resources, confidence, and a willingness to receive.

It might be a good idea to make a list of everything you seek in an ideal romantic relationship, then ask yourself about each item on that list: "Do I really want it? Does it fit within my broader life choices? How important is it in relation to my other desires?" And, if that desire affirmatively makes it through those three questions, ask "What's the best way of getting it?"

> *I require three things in a man:*
> *he must be handsome,*
> *ruthless, and stupid.*
>
> DOROTHY PARKER

Rather than finding one person who's a gourmet cook and likes to go to movies, why not make friends with a gourmet cook *and* a moviegoer? Or join a gourmet society and a movie club. You'll have enough eating, watching, and talking about food and film to more than fulfill these needs. The desire for a workout partner *and* a writing partner is more easily found in two people than in one (unless you live in L.A.). Your dual desires to attend peace rallies and take part in reenactments of major Civil War battles might be best understood by two different comrades in arms.

You may find that some of your desires are best fulfilled *alone*. Meandering through junk shops, reading, and meeting new people are but three examples of satisfying, stimulating, and sometimes challenging activities that are often best done without a partner.

Although it might be *nice* to do things with others, it is far better to do them alone than not to do them at all. In addition, the best way to meet people who have interests in a particular activity is to go where people do that activity. On one of your junk-shop expeditions you may find the perfect lampshade and the perfect junk-shop buddy.

And then there will be those activities that are best left to the professionals—health care, financial advice, automobile maintenance, and house cleaning. "But these things cost money," some protest. "If I were in a relationship, I would get all these things for free." Why do people think romantic relationships don't cost money? They either cost you money, or, if you're getting some financial or material benefit from the relationship, it is costing you time and talent that, if properly marketed, would probably net more cash on the open market. The saying, "Two can live as cheap as one," is as inaccurate as it is ungrammatical.

Another advantage to pursuing each desire separately is not just finding the right partner for each desire, but being able to control how often you take part in each activity. Even if you and your partner were to share an affinity for, say, football, you may be content with one game a week, while your partner desires a game a night. This person watches reruns of games already viewed. Between still, slow motion, and rewind, the typical game lasts five hours. In a romantic relationship, watching football may turn from passion to solemn duty. If, on the

> *You will become as small as*
> *your controlling desire;*
> *as great as*
> *your dominant aspiration.*
>
> JAMES ALLEN

other hand, all you have is a football relationship, your cheering voice and six-pack are interchangeable with anyone else's—you are free to come and go as your gridiron desires dictate.

Which bring us to sex.

Love is the answer,
but while you are waiting for the answer,
sex raises some pretty good questions.

WOODY ALLEN

*Wink, wink,
nudge, nudge,
say no more,
know what I mean ?*

ERIC IDLE
MONTY PYTHON'S FLYING CIRCUS

Sex

Most people can see—or know through hard-won experience—that finding a lover who is everything from cook to career counselor is not a reasonable goal. Dividing one's great need for a Significant Other into smaller, more easily met desires is logical, understandable, and even desirable.

Until it comes to sex.

Sex, after all, is what makes a romantic relationship a romantic relationship; it's not a friendship, partnership, or cohabitationship. The one desire that *cannot* be removed from the equation is sex. "Only someone who meets all the other relationship requirements gets to have sex with me" (or, for some, "Only those who meet all the sexual requirements get to have all the other relationship perquisites"). Therefore, sex cannot be separated out and discussed as an individual desire. In fact, the entire subject of sex is entirely too private, too sacred—so let's not talk about it at all.

Oh, let's. I know it's not comfortable for some people to talk about sex, but how can we thoroughly discuss *love* unless we do?

Fortunately, sex lends itself quite well to dividing and conquering desires. Not only can sex be successfully separated from other relationship needs, but it can—with a little effort and honesty—be divided into smaller, eminently more fulfillable, desires itself.

Sex, like love, is subject to any number of definitions. What one desires when he or she desires

> *Were kisses all the joys in bed,*
> *One woman would another wed.*
>
> WILLIAM SHAKESPEARE

sex might include touching (physically, mentally, emotionally, or spiritually), communication, play, pleasure, satisfying curiosity, lust, committing unpardonable sins (if the sex is any good), creation, procreation, spiritual communion, earning a living, healing, being healed, getting to know someone, avoiding getting to know someone, and, of course, orgasm.

If we took the time to explore our desires and made an honest list of what we are looking for when we say or think we are looking for sex, we would probably discover that some of these desires could be met in ways other than conjugal. We would also discover that many of these desires—including orgasm—can be met without another person even being around. If fact, some of these desires are *better* met without the interruptions and intrusions of others.

Which brings us to masturbation. (If the list of what you wanted to get from sex did not include physical pleasure and orgasm, you're welcome to skip the next few paragraphs—or study them very, very carefully.)

While we are a generation or two away from the times when masturbation was so forbidden that children were taught that they would go blind* or that hair would grow on their palms** if they succumbed to such a sinful act, the taboo is still strong. In December 1994, the Surgeon General of the United States, the chief health official of this country, faced with an epidemic of diseases spread by sexual contact, was fired by the president for suggesting that, perhaps, masturbation could be mentioned in sex education classes as a possible alternative to risk-filled intercourse. The surgeon general, of course, was Jocelyn Elders, M.D; the president is Bill Clinton; and the country, appallingly, was not outraged that he fired her. No matter how enlightened we like to think we and our society are, the taboos against sex in general, and masturbation in particular, are firmly in place.

Like picking one's nose, masturbation is some-

---

*To which advanced children countered: "Can't I do it until I need glasses?"

**To which too advanced, nay, *sassy*, children inquired: "If I'm blind, I won't see the hair on my palms, so what's the difference, anyway?"

> *Many mothers are wholly ignorant*
> *of the almost universal prevalence*
> *of secret vice, or self-abuse,*
> *among the young.*
>
> *Why hesitate to say firmly*
> *and without quibble that*
> *personal abuse lies at the root of much*
> *of the feebleness, paleness, nervousness,*
> *and good-for-nothingness*
> *of the entire community?*
>
> DR. J. H. KELLOGG
> THE INVENTOR OF KELLOGG'S CORN FLAKES
> IN A WARNING AGAINST GRAPE NUTS

thing almost everyone has done and most accept that they will probably do again. When *are* we going to accept our humanity? When are we going to accept that masturbation is no more shameful than cooking and eating alone when we don't happen to have someone we'd like to prepare and share a meal with?

I don't know, but I pray that at some point we do. Looking at the direction our culture seems to be heading, however, I have little hope of that prayer being answered soon. What I see looming on the horizon is intolerance, hypocrisy, and the reasonable fulfillment of human needs being viewed as ungodly, immoral, and un-American. But that's another book.*

In the meantime, might I suggest that you ferret out whatever guilt *you* may have about sex—with self or others—so that you can make a clean, clear, logical choice about what you want to do, with whom, and how often—if at all? Until we approach choices as touchy (sorry) as sex with less negative cultural programming, we cannot truly make a choice—we are either deciding not to do because the culture says don't, or deciding to do because the culture says don't and we are the great rebels of the western world. Either way, the conditioning controls us.

This is not a clarion call to licentious behavior by any means. The irony is that when we reduce our guilt about sex, the amount of sex we actually have may diminish. Guilt has a way of making us always aware of something, and though we may say no ten thousand times in a row, the ten-thousandth-and-first time we fall. When we don't feel guilty about something, the only time we think about it is when we are reminded by others or when a genuine personal desire arises. If sex at that moment is inconvenient or inappropriate, putting it off is not difficult—we haven't said no ten thousand unnecessary times before.

On the other hand, those who have been so traumatized by incendiary reports in the media, and who are afraid they'll contract a hideous disease by even having sex with *themselves,* might find that a

---

*Specifically, *Ain't Nobody's Business If You Do: The Absurdity of Consensual Crimes in a Free Society* by yours truly, at your local bookstore or by calling 1-800-LIFE-101.

> *The next time you feel*
> *the desire [to masturbate]*
> *coming on,*
> *don't give way to it.*
>
> *If you have the chance,*
> *just wash your parts in cold water*
> *and cool them down.*
>
> ROBERT BADEN-POWELL
> TO BOY SCOUTS

few facts and a little guilt abatement leads them to an increase in private sexual adventures.

For the nonsexual desires you have when you think of sex, you may find that a partner specifically chosen for that activity—amateur or professional—is as satisfying, if not more satisfying, than even the last three winners of your romantic relationship bake-off.

The desire to be touched, to experience bodily pleasure, and to have muscular tension released in a way that "hurts so good" is often best met by a professional masseur or masseuse. Even an amateur whose focus is on massage (physical and sensual pleasure) rather than sex (orgasm within a certain period of time) can fulfill the desire to be touched.

If you want to do the touching, offer to give someone else a massage. Here the joy of pleasing another in a deeply physical—and often emotional, mental, and spiritual—way can be met without concerning oneself with disease prevention, pregnancy, or sexual attraction. The joy of massage, like the joy of conversation, is that it's the activity itself that counts, not how attractively it's been packaged and presented.

Trading massages with someone—even if you are both learning as you go—can be a delightful way to fill an afternoon or evening. And this being a book on self-love, I am, of course, going to propose that you learn to massage yourself.

You can reach and successfully massage more than eighty percent of your body yourself. Only certain portions of the back don't lend themselves well to self-massage the way human beings are currently designed. (When we send in our requests for the new and improved models, let's all remember to check the box marked HANDS THAT CAN SCRATCH ANYWHERE IT ITCHES. If you can reach it to scratch it, you can massage it.)

Place several layers of blankets or other padding on the floor, cover with an old sheet, pour some olive oil* into a small bowl, put on some soft music (or some passionate, romantic music), and *love* yourself.

Take your time. There's no hurry. Feel free to experiment. If it feels good, don't avoid it (as you

---

*While olive oil may have a slight odor itself, it is the only oil that never turns rancid, so your sheets and blankets don't end up smelling like a cheap diner.

> *The only reason*
> *I feel guilty about masturbation*
> *is that I do it so badly.*
>
> DAVID STEINBERG

may have been trained)—*do it more*. (O, what a rogue and pagan slave am I.) And don't ignore the sore spots—unless you're healing from a physical wound; those sore spots are telling you something: "Yo! We need some loving over here!" Gently but firmly massage around and into the pain *only to the point that it hurts good*. This is a time of self-loving, not a test of your pain endurance.

Throughout the massage, tell yourself, "I love me," or tell specific parts of your body as you massage them, "I love you." You can add the affirmation, "My touch heals me," and, if you choose, move into the spiritual realms of sensual pleasure by reminding yourself that, "God is within me," and "The God within me heals me."

You may want to take a hot bath before or after your massage—or both. Hot baths are excellent for releasing general tension in the body, while massage has a way of releasing deeper, localized tension.

You might want to explore some of the eclectic (some electric) massage paraphernalia on the market. My only recommendation:* make sure you can return it and get a refund. A mechanical device that is deeply satisfying for person A may seem, to person B, not even turned on yet. Conversely, the device that makes person B melt into a pool of bliss, seems to person A like a device used by road construction crews to pulverize concrete. If you don't like a massage device, take it back and try another.

Am I suggesting that you forego sex with others and explore only the pleasures of your own harbor? Not at all. Ironically—as with love itself—when we fulfill the desires that make up the larger desire of sex, sex seems to become even more available.

---

*Other than the overall recommendation that you check with your doctor or health care professional before embarking on any changes in physical self-care if you have a physical illness, are recovering from an injury, or have some other medical condition that might not respond well to massage—especially in its more electro-vibrational modes.

*Early in life
I had to choose
between honest arrogance
and hypocritical humility.*

*I chose
honest arrogance
and have seen no occasion
to change.*

FRANK LLOYD WRIGHT

The Sanctuary

I am going to make a suggestion here that I've made in all of the books of the LIFE 101 SERIES—build a sanctuary. A sanctuary is a delightful way to discover, enhance, and use the remarkable, unique, and fascinating abilities that make you you.

A sanctuary is an inner retreat you build with visualization in your imagination. Here you can discover the truth about yourself, and work to affirm it. ("Make it firm.")

I call it a sanctuary. Some call it a workshop, or an inner classroom. You can call it whatever word gives you the sense of asylum, harbor, haven, oasis, shelter—a place you can go to learn your lessons in peace and harmony.

There are absolutely no limits to your sanctuary, although it's a good idea to put some limits on it. In this way, the sanctuary is a transitional point between the limitations of our physical existence and unlimitedness.

The sanctuary can be any size, shape, or dimension you choose—large and elaborate or small and cozy. It can be located anywhere—floating in space, on a mountain top, by an ocean, in a valley, anywhere. (You are welcome to combine all those, if you like.) The nice thing about the sanctuary: you can change it or move it anytime—instantly.

The sanctuary can contain anything you choose. I'll suggest some things here, but consider this just the beginning of your shopping list. Before giving my design tips (you can consider me an interior de-

> *There is only one admirable form*
> *of the imagination:*
> *the imagination that is so intense*
> *that it creates a new reality,*
> *that it makes things happen,*
> *whether it be a political thing,*
> *or a social thing or a work of art.*
>
> SEAN O'FAOLAIN

signer—with an emphasis on the word *interior*), I'll talk about ways in which you might want to "build" your sanctuary.

Some people will build theirs by simply reading the suggestions: as they read each, it's there. Others might read them over now, and then put on some soft music, close their eyes, and let the construction begin. Still others may want to make this an *active* process. With their eyes closed (and being careful not to bump into too much furniture), they might physically move as each area of the sanctuary is built and used. All—or any combination—of these is, of course, fine.

While reading through my suggestions, you will probably get ideas for additions or alterations. By all means make notes of these, or simply incorporate them as you go. Have I gotten across the idea that this is *your* sanctuary? Okay, let's go.

Entryway. This is a door or some device that responds only to you and lets only you enter. (I'll suggest a way to bring others into your sanctuary in a moment.)

Light. Each time you enter your sanctuary, a pure, white light cascades over you, surrounding, filling, protecting, blessing, and healing you—for your highest good, and the highest good of all concerned.

Main Room. Like the living room of a house or the lobby of a hotel, this is the central area. From here, there are many directions to go and many things to explore.

People Mover. This is a device to move people in and out of your sanctuary. No one ever enters without your express permission and invitation. You can use an elevator, conveyor belt, *Star Trek* beam-me-up device, or anything else that moves people. Let there be a white light at the entry of the mover as well, so that as people enter and leave your sanctuary, they are automatically surrounded, filled, protected, and healed by that white light, and only that which is for their highest good and the highest good of all concerned is taking place.

Information Retrieval System. This is a method of getting any kind of information—providing, of course, it's for your highest good (and the highest good of all concerned) that you have it. The information retrieval system can be a computer screen, a staff of librarians, a telephone, or any

> *The whole difference between*
> *construction and creation*
> *is exactly this:*
> *that a thing constructed*
> *can only be loved after it is constructed;*
> *but a thing created*
> *is loved before it exists.*
>
> G. K. CHESTERTON

other device that will answer your questions.

Video Screen. This is a video (or movie, if you like) screen in which you can view various parts of your life—past, present, or future. The screen has a white light around it. When you see images you don't like or don't want to encourage, the light is off. When the screen displays images you want to affirm, the light glows. (Those who are old enough to remember Sylvania's Halo of Light television know just what I mean.)

Ability Suits. This is a closet of costumes that, when worn, give you the instant ability to do anything you want to do—be a great actor, successful writer, perfect self-lover, eager learner, Master of your Universe; any and all are available to you.

When you're done with an ability suit, just throw it on the floor—ability suits have the ability to hang themselves up.

Ability Suit Practice Area. This is a place you can try new skills—or improve on old ones—while wearing your ability suits. Leave lots of room, because there's an ability suit for flying and another for space travel. In your sanctuary, not even the sky's a limit.

Health Center. Here the healing arts of all the ages—past, present, future; traditional and alternative—are gathered in one place. All are devoted to your greater health. The health center is staffed with the most competent health practitioners visualization can buy. Who is the most healing being you can imagine? That's who runs your center.

Playroom. Here, are all the toys you ever wanted—as a child or as an adult. There's lots of room—and time—to play with each. As with ability suits, you never have to worry about "putting your toys away." They put themselves away.

Sacred Room. This is a special sanctuary within your sanctuary. You can go there for meditation, contemplation, or special inner work.

Master Teacher. This is your ideal teacher, the being with whom you are the perfect student. The Master Teacher knows everything about you (has always been with you, in fact). The Master Teacher also knows all you need to learn, the perfect timing for your learning it, and the ideal way of teaching it to you. You don't *create* a Master Teacher—that's already been done. You *discover* your Master Teacher. To meet your Master Teacher, simply walk over to

> *We must reserve a back shop*
> *all our own, entirely free,*
> *in which to establish*
> *our real liberty and*
> *our principal retreat and solitude.*

MICHEL EYQUEM DE MONTAIGNE
1580

your people mover, ask for your Master Teacher to come forth, and from the pure, white light of your people mover comes your Master Teacher.

(I'll leave you two alone for a while. More uses for the sanctuary later. See you both in the next chapter!)

Where is the love,
beauty and truth
we seek,
But in our mind?

PERCY BYSSHE SHELLEY
1819

*Man's task is to become
conscious of the contents
that press upwards
from the unconscious . . .*

*As far as we can discern,
the sole purpose of human existence
is to kindle a light
in the darkness of mere being.*

C. G. JUNG

Using Your Sanctuary for Loving Yourself

This chapter is but the barest outline—a mere scratching the surface—of the self-loving opportunities to be enjoyed in the sanctuary. Perhaps the most exciting aspect of the sanctuary is that it's *always there*. You carry it around inside you (a moveable feast, Hemingway might have called it—some have called it a portable paradise); you take it with you wherever you go. You may forget to *use* it, but you can't forget to *take* it.

With time and a little practice, you'll find that you can enter your sanctuary more and more quickly. Soon you'll find you won't *even* have to close your eyes to be "in" your sanctuary—your sanctuary need not be a place to go to, but a place to live from.

The single greatest gift in your sanctuary is, of course, your **Master Teacher.** People like to view the Master Teacher in different ways. Some see the Master Teacher as the better part of themselves, a part that is more in tune with the forces of nature, and the repository of wisdom we all contribute to and are welcome to take from (Carl Jung called this the *collective unconscious*). The Master Teacher is aware of what we need to know, and when it would be best for us to learn it (knowing it all *now* is only fun occasionally; we need to forget most of the time so we can keep playing this life-game). Our Master Teacher gives us encouragement, solace,

> *Creative activity could be described*
> *as a type of learning process*
> *where teacher and pupil*
> *are located in the same individual.*
>
> ARTHUR KOESTLER

and nurturing whenever we are willing to open even *that much* to receive it.

Others like to see the Master Teacher as a spiritual being separate from themselves, but so close, caring, and intimate that the distinction between "my will" and "thine" blurs and often disappears. Whether this being is seen as Jesus, the Holy Spirit, Buddha, Mohammed, Krishna, a Guardian Angel, The God Within, Nature, Intelligence, or any other named or nameless form, is just fine.

The role your Master Teacher can play is an important—even essential—one in your loving of self. From one view, your Master Teacher *is* you, loving yourself; from another view, you are loving yourself by remembering to ask your Master Teacher for loving, and then taking the time to let that loving in. Either way, you are central to the kindness, nurturing, and support you receive from your Master Teacher—consider it a part of you loving yourself.

An effective way to use your Master Teacher is (a) ask for what you want, and (b) let it in (let it happen, let it go, let it grow). Another great way of using the Master Teacher is by asking for suggestions on what you might want to ask about, but haven't thought to ask yet.

Don't use the Master Teacher as a replacement for your common sense, intelligence, or free choice, but do remember: the Master Teacher knows an awful lot about you and is definitely on your side. (If you begin relying on the Master Teacher too much for thinking and decisions you should be making yourself, your Master Teacher will let you know.)

Don't feel the need to use your Master Teacher only "when all else fails," as though the Master Teacher were the Red Cross or Jimmy Carter. Keep the Master Teacher nearby. Have an ongoing dialogue. That wise voice you've been talking and listening to all this time (yes, we all do it) might just have been your Master Teacher all along.

I could go on and on about the friendship, comradeship, and, yes, discipleship of your relationship with your Master Teacher, but I've said enough for now. This relationship will, in time, explain itself to you.

Let's take a look at some of the other tools of the sanctuary and how they might be used for self-loving.

> *Light, love, life.*

JOHANN GOTTFRIED VON HERDER
EPITAPH

Second only to the Master Teacher in importance is **light.** This light that surrounds, fills, protects, blesses, and heals you each time you enter or leave the sanctuary, and that provides the same service to all those you invite into your sanctuary, is available not just in your sanctuary, but in all other areas of your life as well.

From a self-loving point of view, one might want to define this light as "the light of my own loving." The loving here is not the emotional love that tries to control the outcome of things, but more the spiritual loving which asks for, affirms, and accepts that the highest good of all concerned will take place in all of life's light-filled situations. From a spiritual point of view, using the light is simply saying "God's will *will* be done," and you are flowing the best you can with it. From a practical point of view, using the light allows you to send your best thoughts, best wishes, and best intentions to the here-and-now and on into the future.

Please, however, don't use the light the way it was used in a cult of my acquaintance. The members (including—and especially—its leader) would ask others to "send the light for . . ." and then say expressly what they wanted the light to do. Those who were particularly clever about terminology would say, "Send the light for the highest good to . . ." and then state what the light should do. This is *not* using the light for the highest good. This is voodoo, black magic, and psychic manipulation.

You can certainly ask for what you want, and desire what you want with a passion greater than the lust Romeo had for Juliet and Juliet had for being in love. But attaching a spiritual light to this desire and turning the spirit's first law (acceptance) into the first law of mammon (demand) corrupts both the power of spirit and the laws of material manifestation.

So, send the light for the highest good of all concerned; accept ahead of time whatever turns out to be for the highest good; and, if you want the result to go a certain way, get busy and *do things* to make that result a reality. It's like the Christian battle cry: "Praise the Lord and pass the ammunition," or the Moslem proverb: "Trust in Allah, but tie your camel."

The **people mover** guarantees you will never be alone (unless you want to be), and you'll never have to spend time with just any available anyone. You might as well have a discussion (or dinner, or watch

> *Each man's memory*
> *is his private literature.*
>
> ALDOUS HUXLEY

a movie) with Albert Schweitzer, Joan of Arc, or Judy Garland—who are all available through the white light of your people mover. You can also consult the great self-lovers of all time and ask them for tips, or even buy a drink for (and they'll need it) some of the great self-haters of history. (You can ask them what went wrong and what they'd do better next time.)

The **information retrieval system** can be used to find information about you, for you. You'll get the information you're looking for—but only if it's for your highest good to get it.

The **video screen** can be used to heal memories from the past and preview the joys of the future. To heal a memory, sit in front of the video screen, having the white light around it not illuminated. Then watch the unhappy, unproductive, and hurtful memory unfold on the video screen. Let it play itself out—but no reruns. When finished, see the white light around the screen glow brightly, and then see precisely the same incident, but this time see it *as you would have liked it to happen*. Let it be *precisely* the way you wanted it—always win in your imagination. This exercise actually replaces painful memories with positive ones. Research has shown that a passionate visualization can produce a memory that has the same power (either positive or negative) in the brain's memory bank as the memory of a real event. There's no need to go *searching* for negative memories to turn positive, but when they surface, you can turn them from negative to positive and let them sink back into the reservoir of memories that make up a large part of "you."

You can use your video screen—along with the **ability suits,** the **ability suit practice area,** and the **playroom**—to see, feel, try on for size, and actually do some of the fun, exciting, and passionate things you would like to have, do, or be.

Your **health center** can be used to heal yourself as well as others (whom you invite in through the people mover and who give their consent). You can also heal whichever parts of you are not quite on the let's-love-ourselves bandwagon.

The **sacred room** is a place to meditate, have meetings with significant beings you either invite in through your people mover, or ones your Master Teacher, thinking you might like to know them, invites in.

> *Creativity can solve
> almost any problem.*
>
> *The creative act,
> the defeat of habit by originality,
> overcomes everything.*
>
> GEORGE LOIS

Some people like to sleep in their sacred room. When they go to bed at night, they close their eyes, come into their sanctuary, pick up the Master Teacher at the people mover, and head for their specially prepared sleeping place in the sacred room.

As I mentioned at the start of this chapter, I haven't even covered the tip of the iceberg of opportunities for self-loving in your sanctuary. From a certain perspective—and a very accurate one—*any* work you do in your sanctuary is self-loving.

*No man that does not see visions
will ever realize any high hope
or undertake any high enterprise.*

WOODROW WILSON

I might repeat to myself,
slowly and soothingly,
a list of quotations beautiful
from minds profound—
if I can remember
any of the damn things.

DOROTHY PARKER

Affirmations

Affirm means to make firm, solid, more real. Thoughts—not very solid—when repeated over and over, become more and more firm. They become feelings, behaviors, methods, experiences, and things. What we think about, we can become.

We affirm all the time. Sometimes we affirm negatively; sometimes we affirm positively. In the words of Henry Ford, "If you think you can do a thing, or think you can't do a thing; you're right."

I, of course, am going to suggest that you consciously affirm the positive. Many of us already have the unconscious habit of affirming the negative. To change that, I quote Johnny Mercer: "You've got to accentuate the positive, eliminate the negative, latch on to the affirmative."

Affirmations often begin with "I am . . . ." "I am a happy, healthy, wealthy person." "I am joyful no matter what is happening around me." "I am loving and kind." If you're affirming for material things, it's a good idea to start even those with "I am . . . ." "I am enjoying my new house." "I am creative and content in my new career."

Affirmations are best expressed in the present. "I want a new car," affirms *wanting* a new car. What you probably want, however, is the *car.* "I am safely and happily enjoying my beautiful new car." Affirm as though you already have what you want, even though you don't yet have it. (The operative word is "yet.")

No matter how "impossible" something may

> *Love doesn't*
> *grow on the trees*
> *like apples in Eden—*
> *it's something*
> *you have to make.*
>
> *And you must*
> *use your imagination*
> *to make it too,*
> *just like anything else.*
>
> JOYCE CARY

seem, put it into an affirmation and give it a try. Say it, out loud, at least one hundred times before you decide how "impossible" something might be. After one hundred repetitions, you may find yourself quite comfortable with the idea.

You can write affirmations on paper and put them in places you will see them often—on the bathroom mirror, refrigerator, next to your bed, on the car dashboard. You can also record them on endless-loop cassette tapes and play them in the background all day (and night).

A powerful technique is to say your affirmation while looking into your eyes in a mirror. This is especially true of "I love me," or said to yourself, "I love you." All your limitations about whatever you're affirming are likely to surface, but persevere. Outlast the negative voices. Plant the seed of your affirmation deep.

Create affirmations for each of the experiences you want. They can be very simple: "I am content." "I am joyful and calm in the peace of my mind." "I am strong and powerful."

Affirmations work if you use them. The more you use them, the more they work. They can be used anywhere, anytime, while doing almost anything.

It's a good idea to end all your affirmations with ". . . this or something better, for the highest good of all concerned."

The ". . . this or something better . . ." lets ten million come in when you merely asked for a million, and ". . . for the highest good of all concerned" assures that your affirmation is fulfilled in a way that's best for everyone.

Learn to automatically turn all your wishes and wants into affirmations. Then start catching your negative thoughts, switching them around, and making affirmations out of them. By only slightly revising the negative chatter (changing "can't" to "can," "won't" to "will," "hate" to "love," etc.), you can turn all those formerly limiting voices into a staff of in-house affirmation writers.

Another automatic affirmation maker is to revise ads, movie titles, songs, and other media advisories that you only become complete by loving another. "I'll Be Loving You, Always" becomes "I'll Be Loving Me, Always."* "She Loves You" becomes "I Love Me" (Yeah, yeah, yeah!). McDonald's mislead-

> *Thought*
> *takes man*
> *out of servitude,*
> *into freedom.*
>
> HENRY WADSWORTH LONGFELLOW

ing "We Do It All For You!" (do they expect us to believe they don't do it all for *money?)* becomes "I Do It All For Me!" The list is as endless as the media bombardments (which are very close to endless) imploring you to find another to love.

Here are a few affirmations to get you started, but this is a very brief list.

- ❦ "I love me."
- ❦ "God is within me."

---

*Or, perhaps, you prefer George S. Kaufman's variation, "I'll Be Loving You, Thursday."

❧ "God within me heals me."

❧ "I heal me."

❧ "I am worthy of all the good in my life."

❧ "I am one with the Universe, and I have more than I need."

❧ "I am happy that I always do the best I can with what I know and always use everything for my advancement."

❧ "I am forgiving myself unconditionally."

❧ "I am grateful for my life."

❧ "I am loving and accepting myself and others."

❧ "I am treating all problems as opportunities to grow in wisdom and love."

❧ "I am relaxed, trusting in a higher plan that's unfolding for me."

❧ "I am automatically and joyfully focusing on the positive."

❧ "I am giving myself permission to live, love, and laugh."

❧ "I am creating and singing affirmations to create a joyful, abundant, fulfilling life."

❧ ". . . this or something better for the highest good of all concerned."

*I have tried to state
the need we have
to recognise
this aspect of health:
the non-communicating
central self,
forever immune
from the reality principle,
and forever silent.
Here communication
is not non-verbal;
it is like
the music of the spheres,
absolutely personal.
It belongs to being alive.
And in health,
it is out of this
that communication
naturally arises.*

D. W. WINNICOTT, M.D.

Meditate, Contemplate, or "Just Sitting"

In addition to your sanctuary, you might like to try any number of meditative and contemplative techniques available—or you might just want to sit quietly and relax.

Whenever you meditate, contemplate, pray, or "just sits," it's good to ask the white light to surround, fill, and protect you, knowing only that which is for your highest good and the highest good of all concerned will take place during your quiet time. You may want to do your meditation in the sacred room in your sanctuary.

Before starting arrange not to be disturbed. Unplug the phone. Put a note on the door. Wear ear plugs if noises might distract you. (I like the foam-rubber kind sold under the trade names E.A.R., HUSHER, or DECIDAMP.) Take care of your bodily needs. Have some water nearby if you get thirsty, and maybe some tissues, too.

Contemplation is thinking *about* something, often something uplifting. You could contemplate any of the hundreds of quotes or ideas in this book. Often, when we hear a new and potentially useful idea, we say, "I'll have to think about that." Contemplation is a good time to "think about that," to consider the truth of it, to imagine the changes and improvements it might make in your life.

Or, you could contemplate a nonverbal object, such as a flower, or a concept, such as God. The

> *Sit in reverie and watch*
> *the changing color of the waves*
> *that break upon*
> *the idle seashore of the mind.*

HENRY WADSWORTH LONGFELLOW

idea of contemplation is to set aside a certain amount of quiet time to think about just *that*, whatever you decide "that" will be.

Meditation. There are so many techniques of meditation, taught by so many books and organizations, that it's hard to define the word properly.

You might want to try various meditations to see what they're like. With meditation, please keep in mind that *you'll never know until you do it*. We may like to think we know what the effects of a given meditation will be by just reading the description, but I suggest you try it and *then* decide.

Breathing Meditation. Sit comfortably, close your eyes, and simply be aware of your breath. Follow it in and out. Don't "try" to breathe; don't consciously alter your rhythm of breathing; just follow the breath as it naturally flows in and out. If you get lost in thoughts, return to your breath.

Mantras. Some people like to add a word or sound to help the mind focus as the breath goes in and out. Some people use *one* or *God* or *AUM (OHM)* or *love.* These—or any others—are fine. As you breathe in, say to yourself, mentally, "love." As you breathe out, "love." If you don't like synchronizing sounds to breath, don't. It doesn't matter.

It's not so much the *sound,* but the *meaning you assign* to the sound. You may use a mantra such as "Ummmm" just because it sounds good. Or you may say that "Ahhhh" represents the pure sound of God. Because you *say* it does, it will.

Affirmations. Brief affirmations can be used in meditation. "God is within me." "I love me."

Some people think meditation takes time *away* from physical accomplishment. Taken to extremes, of course, that's true. Most people, however, find that meditation *creates* more time than it *takes.* Meditation is for rest, healing, balance, and information. All these are helpful to attain a goal.

One of the primary complaints people have about meditating is, "My thoughts won't leave me alone." Well *naturally*—that's what the mind does; it *thinks.* Rather than fight the thoughts (good luck), you might *listen* to the thoughts for nuggets of information. If a thought reminds you of something to do, write it down (or record it on a tape recorder). Then return to the meditation.

As the "to do" list fills, the mind empties. If the thought, "Call the bank," reappears, you need only

> *God made everything*
> *out of nothing,*
> *but the nothingness*
> *shows through.*
>
> PAUL VALÉRY

tell yourself, "It's on the list. I can let that one go." And you will. It is important, however, to *do* the things on the list—or at least to consider doing them in a nonmeditative state. If you don't, you will continue to think about them, again and again.

When finished meditating, not only will you have had a better meditation, you will also have a "to do" list that can be very useful. One insight gleaned during a few minutes of meditation might save *hours*, perhaps *days* of unnecessary work. That's what I mean when I say—from a purely practical point of view—meditation can make more time than it takes.

Quiet minds cannot be
perplexed or frightened
but go on in fortune or misfortune
at their own private pace,
like a clock
during a thunderstorm.

ROBERT LOUIS STEVENSON

It is not irritating
to be where one is.

It is only irritating
to think one would like
to be somewhere else.

JOHN CAGE

Loneliness vs. Solitude

One of the ways the illusion of romantic love hurts most is when it turns the glory of solitude into the ache of loneliness.* The idea that when we are alone we are missing *so much* by not being with a significant other, causes loneliness.

Of course, almost everyone needs interaction with other human beings. This is natural. Human beings are social animals. What is normal but *not* natural (that is, common but not necessary) is to feel anxious or hurt when not physically near someone we "care about."

The idea that there's "something better" has a way of destroying the moment, and the illusion of romantic love is one of the most popular "something betters" around. Comparing what we have with the imaginary notion of what we could have can cause loneliness.

An even more fundamental root of loneliness is all the negative or "dark" aspects of ourselves—real or imagined—that we have failed to acknowledge and accept. We all have—or are afraid we have—certain thoughts, feelings, and desires we wish we didn't. Some call this the *dark side*, the *shadow self*, or the *Beavis and Butt-head within*. Our culture teaches us to deny our dark side, and pursue the romantic illusion of our "better half" in another. In other words, we ignore what's real while we search

*"Language has created the word *loneliness* to express the pain of being alone, and the word *solitude* to express the glory of being alone."—Paul Tillich

> ¶ *Most human beings use their public life like a visiting card. They show it to others and say, This is me.* ¶ *The others take the card and think to themselves, If you say so.* ¶ *But most human beings have another life too, a gray one, lurking in the darkness, torturing us, a life we try to hide like an ugly sin.*
>
> FEDERICO GARCÍA LORCA

for what's not. Is it any wonder we're confused?

If we take the time to explore our shadow self, we generally conclude: "It's there; it's part of me; I don't plan to act on it; but there it is, so what?" Then we are no longer intimidated by the evil thoughts, feelings, and desires that, from time to time, bubble to the surface.

If we have not taken the time to accept our shadow self, whenever we begin to go within, up pops a shadow. Since we haven't accepted it as part of us, we deny it further and try to suppress it. This gives the shadow self even more power because we've added our fear and resistance to it.

At this point, most people look for a distraction.

A distraction can be anything that will take our mind off this whole shadow business, even momentarily—alcohol, food, drugs, cigarettes, sex, work, exercise, TV, and dozens of others.

One of the best distractions is other people. Other people are so *demanding*. They say something, and we're supposed to respond. They do something, and we're supposed to respond. Or they *don't* say or do something, and we're supposed to respond. All this responding is supposed to happen in "real time"—we are supposed to maintain a steady flow of talking and doing, which is meant to resemble conversation and interaction. All this is so consuming—and distracting.

Quite often it's the distraction and not the interaction we seek when we relate to others.

When we don't have an adequate distraction, the darker side sends more and more hobgoblins, which we sometimes label loneliness. We didn't remember these feelings when engaging with other people, so the solution to this loneliness must be people. (Others determine the solution is alcohol, food, drugs, cigarettes, sex, work, exercise, TV, or any of the other distractions.)

When we become involved with another, sure enough, we are sufficiently distracted from our shadow self to feel "less lonely." Interestingly, this distraction does not have to be positive—arguing, bickering, picking on someone, or being picked on is a just as distracting as being loved, cuddled, coddled, and cared for. This aspect of shadow-self avoidance answers the question: "Why do they stay together? All they do is fight." Fighting—they have

> *Romance and work*
> *are great diversions*
> *to keep you from*
> *dealing with yourself.*
>
> CHER

determined either consciously or unconsciously—is better than loneliness.

The solution to loneliness?

First, accept the idea proposed throughout this book—that you're lover enough for yourself, and you've got the right stuff to call romantic love's bluff. Know that you're the love of your life, and proceed on that knowledge.

Second, accept your dark side. To accept certainly does not mean to act on, propagate, or encourage it. Just know that it's there, that everybody's got one, and accept it.

When you realize that you can think about things without acting on them, and that you can trust your self-discipline enough to not physically hurt others, their property, or yourself, you can let your dark side jabber on without taking any of it seriously—and certainly without having to fear, run away, or distract yourself from it.

In fact, the dark side dialogue can get to be amusing. We can smile at the special tortures we invent for those who cut us off in traffic, relish in the ravishment we have planned for that stranger buying avocados in the supermarket, and feel oh-so-macho in our Rambo-like destruction of the lingerie store that treated us disdainfully.

Is this negative thinking? Of course it is. That's what the dark side does. Those who don't allow themselves to enjoy—or even have—an occasional negative fantasy are probably doing themselves more harm by rigidly denying a portion of themselves than whatever disturbance might be caused by thinking "something nasty."

The mirror concept we discussed in the chapter "Self-Knowledge" can help us see and accept our dark side. All the things we see others doing we don't approve of, we probably have at least *thought* of doing at one time or another. Meditation can also be helpful—as we sit quietly, various portions of our dark side may come to light. No need to resist; just accept them.

The good news about your dark side is that once you have discovered it and accepted it, you can use it in a positive way. By "turning a twist on it," as Barbra Streisand puts it, you can move elements of your dark side into the light.

If you have a desire to snoop, you can become a

> *I think it's very important
> to be positive about
> everything in your life
> that's negative.*
>
> *You can turn a twist on it.*
>
> BARBRA STREISAND

private eye. If your sexual imagination is particularly vivid, you can open your own 900-number sex-talk line. If your fantasies are inventively violent, you could become the next Stephen King.

When we're no longer running from what we call loneliness, we can begin to appreciate the joy of being alone—solitude.

*Pray that your loneliness
may spur you into finding
something to live for,
great enough to die for.*

DAG HAMMARSKJÖLD

To sit alone in the lamplight with a book spread out before you, and hold intimate converse with men of unseen generations—such is a pleasure beyond compare.

KENKO YOSHIDA
1340

Consider what you have in the smallest chosen library: a company of the wisest and wittiest men that could be picked out of all civil countries in a thousand years. The thought which they did not uncover to their bosom friend is here written out in transparent words to us, the strangers of another age.

RALPH WALDO EMERSON

Solitary Pleasures

People often have pity for those who dine alone in a restaurant while reading a book. "What a shame," they say. "They must be so lonely."

No, the one with a book is having dinner with Shakespeare, Oscar Wilde, Gore Vidal, or William F. Buckley, Jr. The one observing the reader, drenched in pity, is having dinner with someone he or she met at Uncle Louie's birthday party.

When we are alone, it is much easier to relate to the great minds and thoughts contained in books, audio tapes, movies, and other media. It's also easier to relate to the great ideas and thoughts in our own mind. It's important to develop an appreciation for ourselves, for the pleasure of our own company. A pro at self-love should seldom give the excuse, "I would have gone, but I couldn't find anybody to go with me." Go alone.

Long walks or quiet meditations can help us clarify our goals and contemplate pathways of fulfillment. Time alone also allows for inspiration—that magical instant in which an idea, discovery, or solution appears in the mind from seemingly nowhere. If you're busy chattering with another over incidentals, your moment of inspiration might get lost in the clamor.

Solitude also allows for creative expression. Whatever we would like to express about ourselves, in whatever form we would like to express it, often requires solitary pursuit. Whether these are professional creations or the pastime of a hobbyist, crea-

> *That I am totally devoid*
> *of sympathy for, or interest in,*
> *the world of groups*
> *is directly attributable to the fact that*
> <u>*my*</u> *two greatest needs and desires—*
> *smoking cigarettes*
> *and plotting revenge—*
> *are basically solitary pursuits.*
>
> FRAN LEBOWITZ

tive expression can lead to some of the more satisfying moments of self-love. (And maybe some money, too.)

Perhaps one of the most enjoyable aspects of solitude is doing what you want when you want to do it, with the absolute freedom (external realities aside) to change what you're doing at will. You may decide to go see one movie, but when you get to the cineplex another movie looks more interesting. You may sit through this movie for half an hour, decide its dreadful, and go to a third movie, which turns out to be terrific.

When it's time to eat, you may have planned on Italian, but a sudden desire for egg foo yung leads you in a more Asian direction. You can go to the

Chinese restaurant, order a small serving of egg foo yung, and still have room for pasta later.

Solitude removes all the "negotiating" we need to do when we're with others. All the kindness and consideration we show to others we can show ourselves. Frankly, when people get used to pursuing traditional couple-oriented activities alone, it's hard to adjust to the what-do-you-want-to-do, I-don't-know-what-do-you-want-to-do form of enjoyment.

Which is why when self-lovers choose to do something with others, those others are more likely to be significant—they have more to offer than your average, run-of-the-mill, if-I'm-not-busy-doing-any-thing-else-that-night-then-I'll-go-with-you compan-ions. This means the time we *do* spend with others tends to be more fulfilling, stimulating, and satisfy-ing.

Not only do we choose better companions, we *are* better companions. Having observed a great deal through our solo explorations, we'll actually have something to *say*. We can make a genuine con-tribution to the conversation, and allow ourselves to be contributed to in return.

Sure, you may want to go certain places with certain people, and that's just fine. Enjoying the pleasures of solitude lets you know that while you may want others, you don't need them, and when you are with others, you are with them because you *choose* to be so.

But far be it from me to tackle the entire subject of solitude *alone*. Here's what some other apprecia-tors of aloneness have had to say:

> *He was the only*
> *really independent person*
> *—boy or man—*
> *in the community,*
> *and by consequence*
> *he was tranquilly*
> *and continuously happy*
> *and was envied by all the rest of us.*

MARK TWAIN
OF TOM BLANKENSHIP,
REAL-LIFE MODEL FOR HUCKLEBERRY FINN

Better to live alone; with a fool there is no companionship.—*The Pali Canon (500–50 B.C.)*

Never less idle than when wholly idle, nor less alone than when wholly alone.
—*Marcus Tullius Cicero (106–43 B.C.)*

When you close your doors, and make darkness within, remember never to say that you are alone, for you are not alone; nay, God is within, and your genius is within.—*Epictetus (50–120)*

They are never alone that are accompanied with noble thoughts.—*Sir Philip Sidney (1580)*

In solitude, where we are *least* alone.—*Lord Byron*

By all means use sometimes to be alone.
—*George Herbert (1633)*

For solitude sometimes is best society,
And short retirement urges sweet return.
　　—*John Milton (1667)*

Solitude, though it may be silent as light, is like light, the mightiest of agencies; for solitude is essential to man. All men come into this world *alone* and leave it alone.—*Thomas De Quincey*

You will never be alone with a poet in your pocket.—*John Adams (1781)*

One of the pleasantest things in the world is going on a journey; but I like to go by myself.
　　—*William Hazlitt (1822)*

When from our better selves we have too long
Been parted by the hurrying world, and droop,
Sick of its business, of its pleasures tired,
How gracious, how benign, is Solitude.
　　—*William Wordsworth (1805)*

I never found the companion that was so companionable as solitude. We are for the most part more lonely when we go abroad among men than when we we stay in our chambers. A man thinking or working is always alone, let him be where he will.
　　—*Henry David Thoreau (1854)*

A solitude is the audience-chamber of God.
　　—*Walter Savage Landor (1775–1864)*

To be human is to have one's little modicum of romance secreted away in one's composition. One never ceases to make a hero of one's self—in private.—*Mark Twain*

The man who goes alone can start today; but he who travels with another must wait until that other is ready.—*Henry David Thoreau*

> *To me, the sea is like a person—*
> *like a child that I've known a long time.*
>
> *It sounds crazy, I know,*
> *but when I swim in the sea I talk to it.*
>
> *I never feel alone when I'm out there.*
>
> GERTRUDE EDERLE
> THIRTY YEARS AFTER BECOMING
> THE FIRST WOMAN
> TO SWIM THE ENGLISH CHANNEL

He travels fastest who travels alone.
   —*Rudyard Kipling*

The strongest man in the world is he who stands most alone.—*Henrik Ibsen (1822)*

Aloneness is inevitable in being human. People cannot accept this. They should be aware of it and use it. It heightens your perceptions.
   —*Edward Albee*

Mrs. Ballinger is one of the ladies who pursue Culture in bands, as though it were dangerous to meet it alone.—*Edith Wharton (1916)*

I have a great deal of company in the house, especially in the morning when nobody calls.
   —*Henry David Thoreau*

Every human being is a divinity and can only be a divinity if there are dark aspects in him as well.
—*Hans Werner Henze*

Solitude gives birth to the original in us, to beauty unfamiliar and perilous—to poetry.
—*Thomas Mann*

If I read a book that impresses me, I have to take myself firmly in hand before I mix with other people; otherwise they would think my mind rather queer.—*Anne Frank*

You are only what you are when no one is looking—*Robert C. Edwards*

She would not exchange her solitude for anything. Never again to be forced to move to the rhythms of others.—*Tillie Olsen*

I've always acted alone. Americans admire that enormously. Americans admire the cowboy leading the caravan alone astride his horse, the cowboy entering a village or city alone on his horse.
—*Henry Kissinger*

I couldn't hit a wall with a sixgun, but I can twirl one. It looks good.—*John Wayne*

What I love is near at hand,
Always, in earth and air.
—*Theodore Roethke*

I have never been able to sleep with anyone. I require a full-size bed so that I can lie in the middle of it and extend my arms spreadeagle on both sides without being obstructed.—*Mae West*

I live in that solitude which is painful in youth, but delicious in the years of maturity.—*Albert Einstein*

*Self-love
depressed
becomes
self-loathing.*

SALLY KEMPTON

Depression

A common reason for not being able to like oneself, much less love oneself, is depression. This reason is far more common than we have been led or would like to believe—of the 15 million people suffering from clinical depression in the United States, more than 10 million don't know it. Oh, they know they're suffering; they are well aware of the love-destroying symptoms in their lives—but they blame them on everything *but* clinical depression, the real cause.

In our language, alas, the word *depression* is used to describe two distinct maladies. One use is to express *disappointment:* "They didn't return my phone calls. I'm depressed." "How depressing—the coffee machine is out of *cafe au lait.*" We also feel this mild kind of depression in life's normal cycle of ups and downs.

The other use of the word *depression* is medical—it describes a physical illness caused by a biological (yes, usually genetic) imbalance in the body.

The simple solution for disappointment depression: Get up and get moving. *Physically* move. Do. Act. Get going.

Depression is often caused by a sense of not having accomplished enough. We question the usefulness of what we've achieved in the past, and doubt our ability to achieve anything useful in the future. Self-doubt robs us of our energy. We feel depressed.

We look at all we want to do. It seems overwhelming. We tell ourselves, "I can't do all this," and instantly fulfill our own prophecy by not even

> *Life is not lost by dying;*
> *life is lost minute by minute,*
> *day by dragging day,*
> *in all the thousand small uncaring ways.*

STEPHEN VINCENT BENÉT

trying. The energy drops even more, and the depression deepens.

When we eventually feel we *must* do something, there seems to be so much left undone from our previous inertia that we become confused. The confusion leads to indecision. The indecision leads to, "Oh, what's the use," and more inaction, which leads to . . . you guessed it.

At some point, the cycle must be broken by action. Do something—*anything*—physical. If the house is a mess, pick up *one thing—any* one thing— and *do* something with it: put it away, throw it out, send it to your brother, donate it to charity, something, *anything*. Pick up one more thing. Continue. Eventually, you will have a clean house. Before "eventually," however, the depression will begin to lift.

Disappointment depression's message is, "Get moving. The energy is here. Use it." When you start to move, the energy will meet your movement. But first, you must move. (We'll be exploring shortly how to set and achieve goals of *your* choosing.)

Medical ("clinical") depression is not caused by disappointment or lack of action, but by a biological imbalance in the chemistry of the brain. This form of depression takes a bit more explaining—there are *so many* misconceptions about it. Here's my story.

Over an almost-thirty-year period, I had attended more personal growth workshops, visited more healers, meditated more hours, taken more vitamins, and not only read but written more self-help books than almost anyone I knew. Nevertheless, I was not happy. I wasn't even satisfied. I wasn't even simply bored.

I was miserable.

By mid-1993, I was ready to try anything—even psychiatry. I called Harold H. Bloomfield, M.D., one of my co-authors on *How to Survive the Loss of a Love,* and told him I wanted to make a professional appointment. I met him at his office. We spoke for an hour. Finally, he said, "Peter, you've been suffering!"

Yeah. That's what I was doing—although I had never applied the word *suffering* to myself. His official diagnosis: depression.

Like many people, I had some serious misconceptions about depression. I didn't *like* depression. I didn't *want* depression. But then, I guess you don't get to pick your disease.

> *There's an old joke:*
> *Two elderly women are at a Catskill*
> *Mountain resort and one of them says,*
> *"Boy, the food at this place*
> *is really terrible."*
>
> *The other one says,*
> *"Yeah, I know, and such small portions."*
>
> *Well, that's essentially how*
> *I feel about life.*
>
> WOODY ALLEN
> OPENING LINES TO *ANNIE HALL*

To my surprise, I learned that depression was a physical illness, a biochemical imbalance in the brain most likely caused by certain *neurotransmitters* (the fluid the brain uses to communicate with itself) being pumped away too soon. When there are too few of certain neurotransmitters, brain function becomes inharmonious, and the complex mental, emotional, and physical manifestations known as depression result.

These manifestations can include a "down" feeling, fatigue, sleep disorders, physical aches and pains, eating irregularities, listening to Julio Iglesias, irritability, difficulty concentrating, feeling worthless, guilt, addictions (attempts to self-medicate the pain away), suicidal thoughts, and my personal favorite, anhedonia.

Anhedonia means "the inability to experience pleasure." The original title for Woody Allen's movie *Annie Hall* was *Anne Hedonia*—the perfect description of Woody Allen's character. It was also the perfect description of my life. Although I had spikes of happiness, nothing gave me pleasure for any length of time. The concept of "just being" was entirely foreign to me. My intensive self-help seeking, since 1965, had been my attempt to obtain the simple enjoyment of living that many people seemed to possess naturally.

All my attempts had been unsuccessful—I had a *physical illness* that prevented even the best-built self-esteem structure from standing very long. In the book Harold and I later wrote, *How to Heal Depression,* the chapter explaining this phenomenon is entitled, "The Power of Positive Thinking Crashes and Burns in the Face of Depression." You can plant all the personal growth seeds you want, but they become like the seeds that fell on the rock in Jesus' parable (Matthew 13:5–6):

> Some [seed] fell on rocky places, where it did not have much soil. It sprang up quickly, because the soil was shallow. But when the sun came up, the plants were scorched, and they withered because they had no root.

That's what depression had wrought inside me: one vast, barren rock garden—without the garden.

I also learned that most depression is inherited. I realized that if I looked around my family tree and saw a lot of nuts, there was a very good chance I was

> *I told my wife the truth.*
>
> *I told her I was seeing a psychiatrist.*
>
> *Then she told <u>me</u> the truth:*
> *that she was seeing a psychiatrist,*
> *two plumbers and a bartender.*
>
> RODNEY DANGERFIELD

not a passion fruit (which is *just* what I thought I was). Since depression is a genetic biological illness, like diabetes or low thyroid, it wasn't lack of character, laziness, or something I could "snap out of"—it would be like trying to snap out of a toothache.

I was ready to consider what the good Doctor Bloomfield recommended I do about my depression.

He explained several options, which included two short-term "talk" therapies (Cognitive Therapy and Interpersonal Therapy), and antidepressants—as in *Prozac.* I, who had been programmed to think drugs were the devil's tool, thought—as many people still do—that Prozac was the devil itself.

The Church of Scientology had done a brilliant job programming the media and, hence, the general public, into believing that not only was Prozac unsafe, but *astonishingly* unsafe. They accomplished this (for whatever reason) by finding a handful of people taking Prozac who had done some aberrant things. Scientology then presented the aberrant behavior of these people as typical of Prozac's side effects. It was a thoroughly imbalanced and unscientific presentation.

More than five million people take Prozac in this country every day—ten million worldwide. Millions more have used Prozac since its introduction in 1987. It is among the safest of all prescribed medications. (No one has ever died from taking Prozac—although hundreds die each year from allergic reactions to penicillin, or from internal bleeding caused by aspirin.)

Still, I didn't like the idea of taking a pill that would—as *Newsweek* pointed out on its cover—give me a different personality. I didn't necessarily like the personality I had, but I also didn't want to become a *Stepford* writer.

Harold explained that antidepressant medications do not give one a new personality. There is no "high" connected to them. They're not tranquilizers, pep pills, or mood elevators. All antidepressants do is keep the brain from pumping away certain neurotransmitters too quickly. This allows the neurotransmitters to rise to appropriate levels, which lets the brain function harmoniously again.

An analogy might be that antidepressants plug a hole in a rain barrel so the barrel can fill. The depression lifts because the brain's naturally produced neurotransmitters are allowed to rise to natural

> *Suffering is not a prerequisite
> for happiness.*
>
> JUDY TATELBAUM

levels. Antidepressant medications, then, don't add a synthetic chemical to the brain that makes one "feel better"; they merely keep the brain from pumping away its own naturally produced neurotransmitters too quickly.

Further, if you take antidepressants and feel better, it's *because you are depressed*. If you take an antidepressant and are not depressed, you won't feel much of anything. In this, antidepressants are like aspirin: if you have a headache and take an aspirin, your headache goes away and you feel better. If you don't have a headache and take an aspirin, you won't feel much different. The good feelings touted so enthusiastically by people taking antidepressants are not caused by the antidepressant medication, but by the lifting of the depression—when a pain you've grown accustomed to goes away, the feeling of just plain "ordinary" can seem like euphoria.

Okay. I was ready. Lay on the Prozac.

Within a week of beginning the medication, I felt not exactly better, but as though the bottom of my emotional pit had been raised. In the past, small setbacks had caused a toboggan ride all the way down to an emotional state best described as "What's the point of living?" In the choice between life and death, I would reluctantly choose life (with about the same enthusiasm as Michelangelo's Adam on the Sistine Chapel receiving the spark of life from God), and crawl back up to "normal" again.

Normal for me, however, was depression. As it turns out, I've had a long-term, low-grade depression since I was three. This depressed state was my benchmark for "normal." On top of this, I would have, from time to time, major depressive episodes—lasting from six months to more than a year. When the two of these played together (that is, played havoc together on me), I had what is known in psychiatric circles as a *double depression* (a fate I would not wish on my worst enemy).

After I'd taken Prozac for two weeks, I felt the floor of my dungeon had risen even higher. By the third week, I felt I had—for the first time—some level ground on which to build my life. I still was concerned how firm it was, so I walked across it lightly, as one does across a piece of land that was once quicksand.

That was the image I had: It seemed as though any good deed, any positive project, any accomplishment I

> *When water covers the head,*
> *a hundred fathoms are as one.*
>
> PERSIAN PROVERB

placed on the quicksand would—like Janet Leigh's car in *Psycho*—slowly, painfully, inexorably sink.

Now I inched a little farther toward the center of my land, seeing how *firma* the *terra* really was. It was a great victory when I could jump up and down in what was once an emotional quagmire and know it was finally safe to build there.

What I built, of course, was up to me: if I built depressing things, my life would still be depressing. But now I had a chance to build something stable, something reliable, something good.

I also began feeling *spiritual* for the first time. I felt connected to God in a solid, unpretentious way. The discovery of this connection was no great "hooray, hooray, I found God," but a slow clarification—

like watching a Polaroid picture develop. It all seemed so natural—and simple.

And—just as so many great teachers had said—the kingdom of God *was* within.

I also found myself simply *enjoying* things: ordinary, everyday, no-big-deal activities were *pleasurable.* I remember sitting in a chair, waiting for a table at a restaurant. I was enjoying just sitting there. I felt so contented, all alone, sitting there, it was almost like being in love.

In fact, it seemed that I *was* falling in love—with myself. The major reason I had been unable to love myself was a biological illness—depression. That's why I've gone on about it in such detail here. I include this information *just in case* you or someone you know is depressed. (The odds are one in five that at some point in your life you will be.)

Are *you* depressed? Well, here's a checklist from the National Institutes of Health. On this checklist they also give symptoms of *mania,* which is the irrational, unpredictable upperswing of manic depression. (I never had mania, but I *did* overachieve as a compensation for the depression—I was trying to "prove" my worthiness by outward achievement. Doesn't work.)

According to the National Institutes of Health:

> A thorough diagnosis is needed if four or more of the symptoms of depression or mania persist for more than two weeks or are interfering with work or family life.

> With available treatment, eighty percent of the people with serious depression—

> *Happiness is always a by-product.*
>
> *It is probably a matter of temperament,
> and for anything I know
> it may be glandular.*

ROBERTSON DAVIES

even those with the most severe forms—
can improve significantly. Symptoms can
be relieved, usually in a matter of weeks.

Symptoms of Depression Can Include

- ❐ Persistent sad or "empty" mood
- ❐ Loss of interest or pleasure in ordinary activities, including sex
- ❐ Decreased energy, fatigue, being "slowed down"
- ❐ Sleep disturbances (insomnia, early-morning waking, or oversleeping)
- ❐ Eating disturbances (loss of appetite and weight, or weight gain)
- ❐ Difficulty concentrating, remembering, making decisions

- ❏ Feelings of guilt, worthlessness, helplessness
- ❏ Thoughts of death or suicide, suicide attempts
- ❏ Irritability
- ❏ Excessive crying
- ❏ Chronic aches and pains that don't respond to treatment

In the Workplace, Symptoms of Depression Often May Be Recognized by
- ❏ Decreased productivity
- ❏ Morale problems
- ❏ Lack of cooperation
- ❏ Safety problems, accidents
- ❏ Absenteeism
- ❏ Frequent complaints of being tired all the time
- ❏ Complaints of unexplained aches and pains
- ❏ Alcohol and drug abuse

Symptoms of Mania Can Include
- ❏ Excessively "high" mood
- ❏ Irritability
- ❏ Decreased need for sleep
- ❏ Increased energy and activity
- ❏ Increased talking, moving, and sexual activity
- ❏ Racing thoughts
- ❏ Disturbed ability to make decisions
- ❏ Grandiose notions
- ❏ Being easily distracted

These symptoms are not "just life." If you've had four or more of them for more than two weeks, or *any* of them is interfering with your work or relationships (including with yourself), a diagnosis is in order.

> *Now I adore my life*
> *With the Bird, the abiding Leaf,*
> *With the Fish, the questing Snail,*
> *And the Eye altering all;*
> *And I dance with William Blake*
> *For love, for Love's sake.*

THEODORE ROETHKE

Even if you checked every box (as I must have—I could have been depression's poster boy), you are not *necessarily* depressed. This is simply a checklist to see if a diagnosis from a physician (an M.D., D.O., or psychiatrist) is in order. Your physician may say you're not depressed, but you do (for example) have low thyroid (which mimics depression symptoms in about twenty percent of the cases). This is why a *physician* should be consulted for diagnosis.

On the other hand, emotional support and the administration of short-term "talk" therapies—such as Cognitive or Interpersonal Therapy—are often best given by psychologists (Ph.D.s or MFCCs).

If you think you *may* have depression and are not yet ready to get a medical diagnosis, please at least read *How to Heal Depression*.*

Depression is now one of the most successfully treated of all major illnesses.

*Available at your local bookstore, or by calling 1-800-LIFE-101.

Every human mind
is a great slumbering power
until awakened by a keen desire
and by definite resolution to do.

Edgar F. Roberts

Choosing and Pursuing
Your Dreams

To a large degree, pursuing what we want—what we *really* want, as in "heart's desire"—is the best way to love ourselves. Going after our goals also determines the number and type of relationships we will have with others.

This advice is the opposite of the common cultural belief that what we have and whom we know determine what we should do. I maintain that you should pursue what you want, get what it takes, and meet the people you must, to make what you want happen.

The next few chapters have been adapted from my books *LIFE 101* and *DO IT! Let's Get Off Our Buts*. They outline the basics of defining and pursuing your heart's desire.

If you are at a major choice point in your life, I suggest you pick up a copy of *DO IT!* and read the whole thing. If you've already read *LIFE 101* and *DO IT!* and know your purpose and Big Dream, you can use these chapters for review, or turn to the chapter "Relationships with Others" (page 323) for cakes and ale. (The boxed quotations between here and there, however, are new.)

Living our dreams—doing what *we* find satisfying, *we* find productive, and *we* enjoy—is one of the best ways I know to love oneself. That, and appreciating what we've already are, have, and are doing, of course.

This is the true joy in life,
the being used for a purpose
recognized by yourself as a mighty one;
the being thoroughly worn out
before you are thrown on the scrap heap;
the being a force of nature
instead of a feverish selfish little clod
of ailments and grievances
complaining that the world
will not devote itself
to making you happy.

GEORGE BERNARD SHAW

What Is Your Purpose?

An important part of loving yourself is knowing your purpose—why you're here; the direction you were meant to travel.

To discover your purpose, get a piece of paper and start listing all your positive qualities. You might want to write each positive quality on separate 3x5 cards. This will make sorting them easier later. If no 3x5 cards are handy, listing the qualities on paper will do.*

Don't be shy listing your positive qualities. This is no time for false modesty. Are you kind? Considerate? Compassionate? Creative? Joyful? Loving? Loyal? Happy? Tender? Caring? Write them down.

A purpose usually begins with "I am . . ." followed by an attitude ("joyful" "happy" "caring") and an action ("giver" "explorer" "nurturer").

On another page (or another set of cards), start listing *actions* you find fulfilling—the positive activities you like doing most. Giving? Sharing? Exploring? Teaching? Learning?

Take some time with this process. Reflect on your life. Explore its motivation.

If you get stuck, call a few friends and ask for suggestions. Tell them you're filling out an application for the Peace Corps. You need help with the

---

*Do pick up 500 or so 3x5 cards the next time you're out. We'll be using them later. If you're someone who tends to put tasks off until "later" and then seldom gets to them, you might want to put down this book and go get some 3x5 cards *now*. While you're out, consider your positive qualities. And have fun!

> *One may not*
> *have written it well enough*
> *for others to know,*
> *but you're in love with truth*
> *when you discover it*
> *at the point of a pencil.*
>
> *That, in and by itself,*
> *is one of the few*
> *rare pleasures in life.*
>
> NORMAN MAILER

questions, "What are your best qualities?" and "What activities give you the most satisfaction?"

You might also go to your sanctuary and ask your Master Teacher for some ideas. Or, go to the video screen and review some scenes of satisfaction, joy, or fulfillment from your life. What were the qualities you embodied in those situations?

Consider the people you admire most. What is it you admire about them? What qualities do they embody? Those same qualities are most likely true about you, too, so write them down.

Eventually, a pattern will emerge on the "Qualities" and the "Actions" lists. Begin grouping qualities and actions under general headings. For you, "Compassionate" might include "caring," "loving," and "kind" while, for another, "Kind" might encompass "compassionate," "loving," and "caring." The idea is not to discover which is "right" from Mr. Webster's or Mr. Roget's point of view, but which resonates most clearly within *you*.

Start to play around with the qualities and actions in a sentence that starts, "I am . . . ." A purpose is short, pithy, and to the point. There's usually room for only one or two qualities and an action. "I am a cheerful giver," "I am a joyful explorer," "I am a compassionate friend."

Please consider my grammatical structure as a starting point. "I am a minstrel of God," "I sing the song of life," or "I serve the planet" are outstanding purposes that don't fit the "I am a [quality] [action]" format. Go to the *spirit* of what a purpose is—the *purpose* of a purpose, if you will—and find your purpose there.

After a while of rearranging qualities and actions, something will click. A voice inside will say, "Yes, this is what I've always done, and this is what I'll always be doing." (This discovery can come with equal parts joy and resignation—joy at seeing that our life has had a direction all along; resignation in noticing it may not be as *glamorous* as we had secretly hoped.)

And that's your purpose.

You might want to place your purpose in a prominent place in your sanctuary—emblazoned on the wall in letters of fiery gold, or, perhaps, on a hand-sewn sampler.

I suggest you not tell your purpose to anyone. That's why I suggested—as a joke, of course—the Peace Corps ruse.*

> *Why be influenced by a person*
> *when you already are one?*
>
> MARTIN MULL

Keeping your purpose to yourself is not so much *secret* as it is *sacred*. Consider it a beautiful plant. Keep the roots (the essence of the purpose) deep within you, and let the world share its fruits.

Please save your lists (stacks) of qualities and actions. We'll be using them later.

**You didn't *really* tell your friends you were joining the Peace Corps, did you? Oh, dear. All right. Well, call them back, and tell them it wasn't the Peace Corps. It was really the Nobel Selection Committee. Yeah, that's it. The Nobel Selection Committee has been asking a lot of questions about you, and you wanted to have a few comments prepared, should you unexpectedly be invited to Stockholm.

There is then a simple answer
to the question
"What is the purpose
of our individual lives?"

They have whatever purpose
we succeed in putting into them.

A. J. AYER

From his cradle to his grave
a man never does a single thing
which has any first and foremost object
but one—
to secure peace of mind,
spiritual comfort,
for himself.

MARK TWAIN

The Comfort Zone

One of the primary reasons people don't love themselves or pursue their dreams is the comfort zone.

The comfort zone is the arena of activities we have done often enough to feel comfortable doing again. For most, this includes walking, talking, driving, spending time with friends, making money in certain ways—all those once-difficult and disturbing activities that we now find easy and comfortable.

Imagine the comfort zone as a circle: Inside the circle are those things we are comfortable doing; outside is everything else. The wall of the circle is not, alas, a wall of protection. It is a wall of discomfort; a wall of limitation.

The *illusion* is that the wall keeps us from bad things and keeps bad things from us. In reality, the bad things get in just fine (perhaps you've noticed). In reality, too, the wall prevents us from getting what we want.

When we do something new, something different, we push against the parameters of our comfort zone. If we do the new thing often enough, we overcome the fear, guilt, unworthiness, hurt feelings, or anger, and our comfort zone expands. If we back off and honor the limitation, our comfort zone shrinks. It's a dynamic, living thing—always expanding or contracting.

When our comfort zone expands in one area, it expands in other areas as well. When we succeed, our confidence and self-esteem increase, and we

> *The man who fears suffering*
> *is already suffering*
> *from what he fears.*
>
> MICHEL DE MONTAIGNE

take that confidence and self-esteem with us into other endeavors.

When we "give in" to our comfort zone, the zone contracts. Our belief that we "aren't strong enough," "can't do it" and are, basically, "not good enough" often prevents us from even *thinking* about approaching "the wall" again for some time.

For some, the comfort zone shrinks to the size of their apartment: they never leave home without anxiety; some people never leave home at all. They sit and watch the news on TV. The news certainly supports the notion that it's a hostile, dangerous place out there, and it's better to stay home (unless a *plane* crashes into your *apartment building!*).

For a few, the comfort zone shrinks to a space

smaller than their own body. We've all probably seen or heard of institutionalized people who are afraid to move any part of their body in any direction. That is when the comfort zone "wins" its greatest victory.

That and suicide. The "it" some people refer to when they "just can't take it anymore" is the need to *constantly* be confronting the comfort zone just to keep it at bay.

Here is one of the great ironies of life: Those who are doing what they want to do and are consciously expanding their comfort zone at every opportunity experience no more emotional discomfort than people who are trying to keep life "as comfortable as possible."

Discomfort—fear, guilt, unworthiness, hurt feelings, and anger—is a part of life. Some people feel discomfort when they press against their comfort zone and make it larger. Other people feel discomfort when they even *think* they *might* do something that gets them even *close* to the (ever-shrinking, in their case) boundary of their comfort zone. *Both feel the same discomfort.*

In fact, people in shrinking comfort zones probably feel more discomfort. They not only feel fear; they also feel the fear of feeling fear; and the fear of the fear of feeling fear; and on and on. The person who develops the habit of moving through fear when it appears, feels it only once. It's the old "A coward dies a thousand deaths, a brave man dies but one."

Some people don't just honor their comfort zone, they *worship* it. When they feel uncomfort-

> *There are hazards in anything one does,*
> *but there are greater hazards*
> *in doing nothing.*
>
> SHIRLEY WILLIAMS

able, they think it is God saying to them, personally and directly, "Don't do this." Some have, in fact, found scriptural references to support their inaction. Not doing new things becomes a matter of *morality*. Those pagans who "don't listen to God" and have the audacity to try new things are not only damned, they should be locked up.

For these dear, uncomfortable souls, I have two quotes: "And the angel said unto them, 'Fear not: for, behold, I bring you good tidings of great joy, which shall be to all people'" (Luke 2:10). Those shepherds who were afraid to "try something new" (listening to an angel in a field) never made it to the manger. And then in 1 John 4:18: "There is no fear in love; but perfect love casteth out fear." This is my favorite method of expanding the comfort zone: Love it all.

In the air conditioning trade, "the comfort zone" is the range of temperatures on the thermostat (usually around 72 degrees) in which neither heating nor air conditioning is needed. It's also called "the dead zone."

That's the result of honoring the comfort zone too much, too often: a sense of deadness; a feeling of being trapped in a life not of our desiring, doing things not of our choosing, spending time with people we don't like.

The answer? Do it. Feel the discomfort, and do it anyway. *Physically move* to accomplish those things you choose.

Learn to love it all.

*Men are not
against you;
they are merely
for themselves.*

GENE FOWLER

Enemies That Aren't

An example of "turning a twist on" emotions we find negative is to turn the limiting emotions of the comfort zone—fear, guilt, unworthiness, hurt feelings, and anger—into expansive energy.

That's all emotions are—energy in motion. It's your energy; you can use it any way you like.

Fear you will find is the same physiological reaction as **excitement.** When we enter—or think about entering—a new situation, our senses sharpen, we get an extra burst of energy, and irrelevant matters are driven from our awareness. If we label it *fear*, we believe this energy says, "Stop!" If we call it *excitement*, we say "Here we go!" And we're off.

Anger is directed at others. What we usually want to change is other people's behavior, and anger—carefully modulated and productively channeled—can do just that. Anger can also be used as the energy to change *us*—specifically our beliefs about the way other people should, must, ought to, have to, and had better behave.

Guilt is **anger** we feel toward ourselves when we don't live up to our own shoulds, musts, have tos, ought tos, and had betters. We can use the energy of guilt to change our actions (occasionally—and especially if the actions physically harm the person or property of another) and for all the rest of the self-judgments (shouldn't have eaten the cake, should've exercised after eating the cake, must read a good book, mustn't waste time channel surfing), we might as well work on modifying our beliefs

> *Hate must make a man productive.*
> *Otherwise one might as well love.*
>
> KARL KRAUS

about our behavior. With enough guilt, do you *really* suppose you're never going to channel surf again? Unlikely. Better eliminate the judgment.

Eliminating the shoulds, musts, have tos, and other inflexibilities we hold against ourselves and others can be one of the most self-loving actions we can take.

Hurt feelings can remind us how much we **care.** We never have hurt feelings unless something we care about is threatened, refused, or taken from us. If we return to *what* we care about and *that* we care, we put our attention on the caring—we can feel the depth of our love and compassion. While I'm certainly not recommending you eliminate the necessary grieving that is part of the mourning process, quite a number of daily disappointments can be turned from hurting to caring if you refocus on the caring. And who is *always* available to care about? You, of course.

Unworthiness can be used to keep us **on track;** to remind us of what we are worthy. If we accept the notion that we can have *anything* we want but not *everything* we want—the limited amount of time we have remaining and the billions of things we *could* want—it's obvious that we're only going to be worthy of a handful of them. The rest—the vast majority—we *are* unworthy of. If we're on a plane to Rome for a vacation, that day we are *not* worthy of Seattle, Tokyo, Bora Bora, or Manhattan Beach. (But we *are* worthy of fettucine Alfredo at the original Alfredo's. Yum!) When we carefully program our worthiness and align it to what we *really* want, then our feelings of unworthiness about all the other desires are simply a friendly reminder: "Your path is over here, not over here."

All those uncomfortable emotions that may be keeping us *from* loving ourselves are, in fact, available as energy *for* loving ourselves. Yum yum.

Anyone can revolt.

*It is more difficult
silently to obey
our own inner promptings,
and to spend our lives
finding sincere and fitting
means of expression
for our temperament
and our gifts.*

GEORGES ROUAULT

Life's Four Basic Areas of Activity

When choosing a dream to pursue, it's good first to consider the four basic areas in which people live. They are

- Marriage/Family

- Career/Professional

- Social/Political

- Religious/Spiritual

Naturally, in the course of a lifetime, people spend some time in each. Looking back, however, most people can say, "Yes, I gave the majority of my time and attention to _____" and mention one of the categories. Sometimes, it's the area they *wanted* to spend most of their time in. Other times, they spent their life in an area other than the one closest to their heart.

In choosing *now* which area you feel most drawn to, you can either (a) spend more time in that area, or (b) realize that the conflict you feel ("I really want to do this, but I think I *should* do that") is from programming other than your own. Now is a good time to start reprogramming yourself so that the goals you follow are your own.

Here's where the "I want it all" syndrome comes in. We somehow think we're *entitled* to fulfill a *significant* goal from *each* of the four categories. All at once. Sorry. I haven't seen it. You can have *any*

> *Dear United States Army: My husband asked me to write a recommend that he supports his family. He cannot read, so don't tell him. Just take him. He ain't no good to me. He ain't done nothing but raise hell and drink lemon essence since I married him eight years ago, and I got to feed seven kids of his. Maybe you can get him to carry a gun. He's good on squirrels and eating. Take him and welcome. I need the grub and his bed for the kids. Don't tell him this, but just take him.*

HAND-DELIVERED IN 1943
BY AN ARKANSAS MAN
TO HIS DRAFT BOARD

category you want, but you can't have *every* category you want.

Life is easier if one faces this hard reality sooner rather than later.

You *can* spend equal amounts of time in each category, but, if you do, don't expect to go very far in any of them. You will live "a balanced life." People will remark, "My, what a balanced life you live."

If, while you're imagining this, a part of you says, "I don't want a balanced life! I want to be a rock star!" (Career/Professional) or "All I care about is my family!" (Marriage/Family) or "What difference does a balanced life make if we can't breathe the air?" (Social/Political) or "This world is but the shadowlands; the greater world is beyond!" (Religious/Spiritual), then perhaps you're not looking for the balanced life after all.

The narrower your goal—and the more fully you supply that goal with your time, energy, and resources—the farther you'll go and the faster you'll get there. Think of a rocket. All its energy is pinpointed in one direction, and it can zoom off to distant planets.

The downside of rocket travel? You can't bring your house *and* your family *and* report for work on time *and* save the whales *and* take all your religious and spiritual books *and* . . . . Very little fits in the capsule of a rocket. If, however, seeing the moon close-up and in-person is your heart's desire, letting go of all but "very little" is the price you must pay.

"All right. I'll settle for *pictures* of the moon."

Much less investment is required for that. You can even have a *video* of the moon. In color. Let go, however, of the dream of seeing the moon in-person and up-close. Letting that dream go will free up energy you can put toward the dream you *do* choose to achieve.

Let's take a look at each of the four basic areas of activity. Along the way, I'll do what I can to dispel a few of the myths that have grown around each.

Marriage and Family

The myths about marriage and family are omnipresent in our culture.

As we've explored, the mythical scenario goes something like this: You are trudging along in life—lonely, but coping. Some Enchanted Evening (across

> *If it is not mere rhetoric*
> *and you really mean what you say*
> *when you say,*
> *"I will do anything you want me to do!"*
> *then let us have a real though minor trial:*
> *will you learn shorthand*
> *as soon as possible?*
>
> *It is a skill worth having anyway.*
>
> DELMORE SCHWARTZ
> TO ELIZABETH POLLET

a crowded room) you meet The Perfect Stranger (as opposed to a total stranger). Fade in music. Fade out loneliness. You are lifted to the pinnacle of bliss, where you and Prince Charming or Cinderella live happily ever after. The end.

This is the most popular version of the larger, underlying myth that says things and people outside ourselves make us happy. ("You made me love you, I didn't want to do it . . .")

In fact, *we* make us happy. ("If you are lonely when you are alone," cautioned Jean-Paul Sartre, "you are in bad company.") The joy we see in others is a reflection of the joy in ourselves. We feel uncomfortable, however, giving ourselves credit for our own joy. It's easier to say, "You're wonderful, and I'm so happy you're with me," than to say, "I'm wonderful, and I'm so happy to be me." The first version may be easier to *say*, but it's not (a) honest, and (b) easy to live with.

It's not easy to live with because, if we feel happiness only when the other person is around, then we have to keep that other person around in order to be happy. If that person happens to be lost in the same illusion, that's called "being in love," and everything is hunky dory—for a while. (As Cher observed, "The trouble with some women is that they get all excited about nothing—and then marry him.")

Eventually, no matter how hard we try to keep up the facade, one partner or the other will peek behind it and see the Dark Side, which is not at all lovable. "He loved me absolutely," wrote Frieda (Mrs. D. H.) Lawrence, "that's why he hates me absolutely."

The Dark Side is, of course, only something we see in another that we don't like about ourselves, and, again, are not honest enough to admit. If A sees B's Dark Side, but B fails to see A's Dark Side, it's Dump City. B sings a medley of torch songs and A cries, "Free Again!" If both see it at once, the perfect lovers become perfect enemies.

Which brings me to children. Children are a twenty-four-hour-a-day commitment, for a minimum of eighteen years—probably longer. With children, you can learn something very important: how to give for the sheer joy of giving. If you give to children with any hope of return, you're inviting misery all around. ("Before I was married I had

> ¶ *The whole point of marriage is to stop you getting anywhere near real life.* ¶ *You think it's a great struggle with the mystery of being.* ¶ *It's more like being smothered in warm cocoa.* ¶ *There's sex, but it's not what you think.* ¶ *Marvellous, for the first fortnight. Then every Wednesday.* ¶ *If there isn't a good late-night concert on the Third.* ¶ *Meanwhile you become a biological functionary.* ¶ *An agent of the great female womb, spawning away, dumping its goods in your lap for succour.* ¶ *Daddy, daddy, we're here and we're expensive.*
>
> MALCOM BRADBURY

three theories about raising children," John Wilmot, the Earl of Rochester, wrote. "Now I have three children and no theories.")

In fact, that's one of the primary lessons one learns—not just from children, but from intimate relationships of all kinds—how to give.

The myth is that marriage is for *receiving*. It's not. It's for giving. ("Marriage is not merely sharing the fettucini," Calvin Trillin explained, "but sharing the burden of finding the fettucini restaurant in the first place.")

But don't take my word for it. Ask anyone who's been in a successful relationship for, oh, at least two years. They'll almost certainly describe themselves as *giving*, with no thought of return. If they go on and on about how much fun it was to *receive*, you're probably talking to Zsa Zsa Gabor.

(When Zsa Zsa was on a call-in radio show, a caller asked, "I want to break up with a man, but he's been so nice to me. He gave me a car, a diamond necklace, a mink stole, beautiful gowns, a stove, expensive perfumes—what should I do?" Without having to think, Zsa Zsa said, "Give him back the stove.")

Another cultural myth is that we are somehow *incomplete* if we do not reproduce. This notion may have had some validity when being fruitful and multiplying was necessary for a species or tribe to continue. Today, however, one of the great problems in the world is overpopulation. Let those who really *want* to reproduce reproduce (and that includes providing the eighteen-year environment in which the reproductions can grow into functioning, creative, healthy humans). Those who want to leave their legacy in another way can feel free to do so.

Another value of relationships is learning about *ourselves*—the good, the bad, the beautiful, and the ugly. Marriage is like a dinner with dessert first. The falling in love portion shows us the beauty within us. Everything else shows us everything else. It's a package deal. When the Dark Side presents itself and says, "I'm in you, too," many people panic.

"Wait a minute. This isn't part of the contract."

"Yes, it is. For better or for worse. This is worse."

"This is *the worst*. Where's the lovey-dovey stuff?"

> *The most fatal illusion*
> *is the settled point of view.*
>
> *Since life is growth and motion,*
> *a fixed point of view*
> *kills anybody who has one.*
>
> BROOKS ATKINSON

"Maybe that bird will return when you learn to love this one."

"I have to learn to love it?"

"You only *have to* learn to *accept* it. Loving it, however, feels better."

People seldom want to face the Dark Side of themselves. Instead, they (choose one or more)

1. Deny it's a mirror and pretend it's the other person. (One must be careful not to strike out too severely at a mirror, for, as we all know, if you break a mirror, it's seven years bad luck—perhaps in jail.)

2. Pretend *really hard* that everything is all right, and "play house." ("Welcome to *At Home with the Ostrich Family*. Here's mother, Heroic Pretender; and father, General Denial. Here are their children,

Make Believe, Gloss Over, and Feign Affection. Don't they all look *happy*? The Ostrich Family!")

3. Realize that the reflected Dark Side they see in the mirror is true about themselves and hate themselves even more.

4. Run!

For those looking for an intensive workshop in self-discovery, self-acceptance, and the perfect place to learn the joy of giving—like it or not—Marriage/Family is an area of life to consider.

(If you thought I was perhaps too hard on marital bliss, let me close with a romantic thought from Britt Ekland: "I know a lot of people didn't expect our relationship to last—but we just celebrated our two months anniversary.")

Career and Professional

Did you ever hear parents placing a curse on their child? "Someday, something's going to straighten you out!" That's what a career is—The Great Straightener.

Next to gravity, there's very little as constant as the business world—it will drag you down if you slip too often, or hurl you to the moon if you understand how to use it. (Most of the energy used in traveling to the moon and back was the gravitational pull of the moon and Earth.) Wernher von Braun found the business side of putting a man on the moon more difficult than the functional side. "We can lick gravity," he said, "but sometimes the paperwork is overwhelming."

A job is what you have when you want to take

> *Music is my mistress,*
> *and she plays second fiddle*
> *to no one.*
>
> DUKE ELLINGTON

the money to some other area of life in order to buy the necessities. Someone whose primary focus is marriage, for example, leaves the marriage only long enough to make the money to support the marriage—baby needs a new pair of shoes and all that. That's a job.*

You have a *career* or *profession* when what you love doing most is what you also get paid for doing. As Noel Coward said, "Work is much more fun than fun." Or, as Richard Bach remarked, "The

---

*Not that staying home and working isn't a job. To illuminate, here's Roseanne: "As a housewife, I feel that if the kids are still alive when my husband gets home from work, then hey, I've done my job. When Sears comes out with a riding vacuum cleaner, then I'll clean the house."

more I want to get something done, the less I call it work."

"But I am an artist," some may say. "I only want to create." If you plan to get paid for creating, then you're in business. "But someone will discover me and take care of all that." Right, and if you have nothing to wear to the ball, your fairy godmother will supervise the mice and the birds in making you a gown.

The days of being "discovered" in the arts went out with Diaghelev. Artists—and that includes actors, singers, writers, dancers, musicians, painters, and so on—must become their own supporters, must champion their own cause. To succeed, they must become patron *and* protégé in one. In other words, if you're a creative person, you must create your own creative outlet. And that means being in business.*

The secret of success in a career? Same as success in any other area. As John Moores explained, "Work seven days a week and nothing can stop you." Not only is success hard work; it's hard, *challenging* work. "If you have a job without aggravations," Malcolm Forbes pointed out, "you don't have a job."

One must, however, not just work *hard*. One must work *smart*. As the saying goes—the efficient person gets the job done *right;* the effective person

---

*In 1988, twenty publishers turned down *You Can't Afford the Luxury of a Negative Thought*, so I published it myself. I then published all the books in the LIFE 101 SERIES myself, because I realized there's a lot more to getting a book into a reader's hands than merely writing it.

> *Pitt the younger was*
> *a great British Prime Minister.*
>
> *He saved Europe from Napoleon,*
> *he was the pilot who weathered the storm.*
>
> *I don't know whether*
> *he'd have done it any better or quicker*
> *had he been married.*
>
> EDWARD HEATH

gets the *right job done*. "The really idle man gets nowhere," Sir Heneage Ogilvie observed. "The perpetually busy man does not get much further."

Of course, a career is not for everyone. Lily Tomlin said, "The trouble with the rat race is that even if you win, you're still a rat."

And, yes, in addition to long hours and hard work, each career has its Dark Side. "The price one pays for pursuing any profession or calling," James Baldwin explained, "is an intimate knowledge of its ugly side."

When one peeks through the glamour, one sees reality, and one may not like it. As Fred Allen said, "When you get through all the phony tinsel of Hollywood, you find the genuine tinsel underneath."

David Sarnoff remarked, "Competition brings out the best in products, and the worst in people."

One *especially* may not like a career's Dark Side when one remembers the mirror—the things we don't like about our career are also what we don't like about ourselves. Is your career insincere? Dishonest? Heartless? Gulp. Behold, the mirror.

If one is willing to see a career as a great, big mirror (career and mirror—they even rhyme, if you pronounce them with a vague Southern accent), there's a lot to learn—facts most people don't want to learn about themselves.

Rather than looking in either the relationship or career mirror, some spend time looking in one until it becomes uncomfortable, then run off to look in the other. Back and forth, endlessly.

The career vs. marriage struggle has been going on since the caveperson who invented the first wheel decided to open Wheels R Us.

One side of the struggle is expressed by George Jean Nathan: "Marriage is based on the theory that when a man discovers a brand of beer exactly to his taste he should at once throw up his job and go to work in a brewery."

Representing the other side of the debate, Bertrand Russell: "One of the symptoms of an approaching nervous breakdown is the belief that one's work is terribly important."

"Can't I have both a career and a marriage?" Well, some can. And some can juggle seven balls while eating a tuna fish sandwich.

What happens at the end of a long, successful career? You'll be glad you chose career over every-

> *Sexual harassment at work —*
> *is it a problem*
> *for the self-employed?*
>
> VICTORIA WOOD

thing else, brimming with pride over all you've accomplished, right?

Well . . .

T. S. Eliot, poet, Nobel Laureate—but better known as the lyricist for *Cats*, heaven help his memory—wrote,

> As things are, and as fundamentally they must always be, poetry is not a career, but a mug's game. No honest poet can ever feel quite sure of the permanent value of what he has written: he may have wasted his time and messed up his life for nothing.

And Sir Thomas More, after fifteen years of practicing law, wrote of an ideal future, *Utopia,*

"They have no lawyers among them, for they consider them as a sort of people whose profession it is to disguise matters." Or, as Robert Frost put it, "By working faithfully eight hours a day, you may eventually get to be a boss and work twelve hours a day."

Social and Political

If the sentence, "I love humanity, it's people I can't stand," fits you, perhaps you should consider a life of social change and political action.

"The only thing necessary for the triumph of evil," Edmund Burke wrote two hundred years ago, "is for good men to do nothing." The world has any number of good people right now, with the dream deep in their hearts to make changes for the better. The problem is not that they're doing *nothing;* the problem is that they're doing *something else.*

People who are naturally drawn toward social action or politics are often repelled by its name.

Here is an area of activity where the *reputation* is worse than the *reality*—a sort of reverse glamour.

"I used to say that politics was the second oldest profession," said Ronald Reagan in 1979, "and I have come to know that it bears a gross similarity to the first." The following year he won the presidency.

"Nobody could sleep with Dick," Pat Nixon revealed. "He wakes up during the night, switches on the lights, speaks into his tape recorder, or takes notes—it's impossible."

John Updike had this explanation for the inconsistency of our leaders: "A leader is one who, out of madness or goodness, volunteers to take upon him-

> *"Even though the labels <u>stripper</u>*
> *and <u>congressman</u>*
> *are completely incongruous,*
> *there was never anything*
> *but harmony in our hearts.*

FANNE FOX
("THE ARGENTINE FIRECRACKER")
ABOUT HER RELATIONSHIP WITH
CONGRESSMAN WILBUR MILLS

self the woe of the people. There are few men so foolish, hence the erratic quality of leadership in the world."

And yet, with all the bad written about it, some do have a few good words for and about the art of politics.

"Public life is regarded as the crown of a career, and to young men it is the worthiest ambition," said John Buchan. "Politics is still the greatest and the most honorable adventure."

"Politics," Gore Vidal wrote, with his own enticing twist on Buchan, "is the grim jockeying for position, the ceaseless trading, the deliberate use of words not for communication but to screen intention. In short, a splendidly exciting game for those who play it."

"If you're going to play the game properly," cautioned Barbara Jordan, "you'd better know every rule."

"True leadership must be for the benefit of the followers," wrote Robert Townsend in *Up the Organization*, "not the enrichment of the leaders." Townsend was speaking of the business world, but it applies to the political world as well.

You may not always be popular, even among those you are helping. Harry Truman asked, "How far would Moses have gone if he had taken a poll in Egypt?"

The great social causes that capture the hearts of men and women do not necessarily involve politics. They do, however, involve courage, sacrifice, commitment, and selfless giving—the most challenging aspects of marriage and career combined.

There are, however, inner benefits. "The great use of life is to spend it for something that will outlast it," William James wrote.

And make no mistake about it: we make social changes because, over time, it makes *us* feel better. We may not appreciate the day-to-day tilting at windmills, but we prefer that to day-by-day observing a condition we know we could somehow make better, get worse.

People often think a social problem is too great and they are too small. I suggest: If drawn to do it, do it. "What one has to do," Eleanor Roosevelt pointed out, "usually can be done."

The reward is the joy of giving, the satisfaction of following your heart's desire, and, perhaps, someone will say of you what Clare Boothe Luce said of

> *When you make*
> *a world tolerable*
> *for yourself*
> *you make*
> *a world tolerable*
> *for others.*
>
> ANAIS NIN

Eleanor Roosevelt: "No woman has ever so com-
forted the distressed—or distressed the comfortable."

Religious and Spiritual

Here I tread softly. In *LIFE 101*, I put all the religious and spiritual beliefs—from Catholicism to An-
glicanism to agnosticism to atheism—in an area I
called The Gap.

The contents of anyone's Gap is between the individual and the contents of his or her Gap. I don't
get involved with The Gap in these books because
the tools I discuss work regardless of what's in anyone's Gap, just as a cookbook or car repair manual
works for Baptist and Buddhist alike.

In discussing the areas of life's activity, however, I must touch on an area some people are strongly drawn to—religion and spirit.

There is an interesting ambivalence to religion and spirituality in our culture. On one hand, if people have no beliefs, they are thought odd. On the other hand, if they devote all their time to the understanding and worship of God, they, too, are thought odd.

As with politics, people may hesitate pursuing spirit full time because religion has been so, well, shall I say (tap, tap, tap) has made God to look, uh, um (tap, tap, tap—that's me tap dancing while arriving at a diplomatic, nonjudgmental way of saying this), perhaps some people's behavior has not cast the Deity in the best possible light.

For example, the chief executive of Coca-Cola described his company, "It's a religion as well as a business." (By the way, do you know that the taste of cola is a combination of three familiar flavors? Which three? If you want to guess, I'll wait for a bit before telling you.)

Others seem to use God as some great bellhop in the sky—"give me this, send me that, take this away." Dorothy Parker parodied these people when she wrote, "Oh God, in the name of Thine only beloved Son, Jesus Christ, Our Lord, let him phone me *now.*"

All of this—and I haven't even *mentioned* televangelists and their traumas—may have made traditional religion seem a little strange, even to those who feel a calling. My advice, as always: follow your heart.

Of course, there are those who think they *should*

> *Einstein was a man who*
> *could ask immensely simple questions.*
>
> *And what his work showed*
> *is that when the answers are simple too,*
> *then you can hear God thinking.*
>
> JACOB BRONOWSKI

spend all their time worshiping God because, after all, God is God and isn't that what I'm *supposed* to do? And, even though these people are off pursuing a goal in another area of life, they feel *guilty* for not *praying* more—as though God were an overanxious mother who hasn't had a phone call in a month. (Although, if that is your image of God, far be it from me to de-Deify you.) Might I suggest to these people that they let their good works in whatever field they choose glorify God? (Cola, by the way, is made up of these three flavors: citrus [lemon or lime], vanilla, and cinnamon.)

And for those who are feeling the Ultimate Unworthiness—not worthy to serve God—I offer you this from Phyllis McGinley:

The wonderful thing about saints is that they were human. They lost their tempers, scolded God, were egotistical or testy or impatient in their turns, made mistakes and regretted them. Still they went on doggedly blundering toward heaven.

Fun and Recreation

I'm not sure whether all work and no play made Jack a dull boy, or whether Jack was a dull boy to begin with, so, dullard that he was, he worked too much. Either way, fun and recreation are a necessary part of an undull life.

When I say *recreation*, I mean it in the lighter sense of recreation (tennis, boating, going to the movies), as well as in the deeper sense—*re-creation*. What do you do to "recreate" yourself? This might include meditation, retreats *(re-treats)*, prayer, spiritual work, rest, pilgrimages, massage, silent time— whatever activities recharge your batteries in a deep and powerful way.

I didn't include Fun/Recreation as a basic area of life because I assume this is an area people will want to enjoy no matter what other area they choose. To use the battery analogy, Fun/Recreation charges the batteries; Marriage/Family, Career/Professional, Social/Political, and Religious/Spiritual are the ways in which the batteries are used.

It's important to realize, however, that the endless pursuit of fun and recreation *in and of themselves* is not very fulfilling. In fact, it's something of a curse. When one pursues pleasure *all the time,* the

> *I would rather score a touchdown*
> *than make love to the prettiest girl*
> *in the United States.*
>
> PAUL HORNUNG

pursuit of pleasure becomes work—it's a job. If pleasure is one's job, then where does one go to recharge the batteries for more work? The pleasure *is* the work. Hence, perhaps, the old saying about not mixing business with pleasure.

Fun and recreation form a stable base for fulfilling one's dreams—they're just not a very good dream all by themselves.

I don't say we all ought to misbehave,
but we ought to look as if we could.

ORSON WELLES

The common idea
that success spoils people
by making them vain,
egotistic,
and self complacent
is erroneous—
on the contrary
it makes them,
for the most part,
humble, tolerant and kind.
Failure makes people
bitter and cruel.

W. Somerset Maugham

What Have You Accomplished?

In the next two chapters, I'll ask you to do some writing, as well as some remembering and observing. If you're reading this book for information now and plan to do the "work" later, when you return to do the work, please begin with the chapter "What Is Your Purpose?" and then return to this one.

In doing this exercise, you might want to use 3x5 cards, as that eliminates the need for rewriting. It's not necessary for this exercise, and you'll need a lot of them—200 to 300, probably. If you're low on 3x5 cards (fewer than 300), please save them for the exercises in the chapter "What Do You Want?"

So, what have you accomplished? As things come to mind, set this book aside and write them down (one per card). I'll make some comments to jog your memory, but when it's jogged, write for a while, and then return for some more jogging.

What have you accomplished? What have you achieved? What things did you want and go out and get? They may be a part of your life now, or they may be long gone. Either way, write them down.

Cars? Jobs? Apartments? Stereos? Furniture? You don't need to list every piece of clothing or can of beans you ever bought, but if some special purchases or exceptional dinners come to mind, write them down.

What about schooling? Did you get a high school diploma? What degrees did you obtain? Perhaps

> *An idea isn't worth much*
> *until a man is found*
> *who has the energy and ability*
> *to make it work.*
>
> WILLIAM FEATHER

you're prouder of the degrees you *didn't* receive. What about night classes, workshops, seminars, or other less traditional forms of education? Have you learned a language? How to change your own oil? Cook? Play ball (any ball)? Dance? Sing? What are your hobbies? Where have you traveled? What about the books you've read? Plays you've seen? Miniseries you've lived through? Tapes you've listened to?

What about people? Of whom did you say, "I want this person for a friend/lover/boss/employee/teacher/student/roommate/wife/husband/etc.," and got them? Even if you didn't initiate the relationship, for every relationship you've ever had, you had to do *something*, even if it was not saying no.

The fact that a relationship, job—or anything

else—may have *ended* poorly doesn't mean it shouldn't be on your list. If it was something you wanted and you got, that counts. Much of our growth comes from getting what we want and finding out we don't want it after all. Even if *they* are the ones who decided the relationships were not what they wanted, include those relationships on your list, too. You had them for a time, and the only difference between a happy ending and an unhappy ending is where they put the closing credits. Go to the happy time, consider it an achievement, and write it down.

What about social or political goals? Did your candidate win? Did the proposal you favored pass? Even if you did nothing more than *vote* for it, that's better than half the people in the United States do in any election. What giving—directly, or through organizations—have you done?

Yes, this is a lot of remembering and a lot of writing. That's the point. We tend to forget what we've accomplished; we tend to forget how much we have created; we tend to forget how powerful we are.

How about family? Did you create any children? What have you done for members of your family? Perhaps *leaving* a family situation that wasn't doing *anyone* any good was a major achievement.

What about health? What illnesses have you successfully recovered from? What changes in your body image have you made? Do you exercise? *Have* you exercised? Take vitamins? Had body work of any kind done? What bad habits have you overcome (even temporarily)? Have you been in therapy?

> *Creativity is merely*
> *a plus name*
> *for regular activity . . .*
> *any activity becomes creative*
> *when the doer cares*
> *about doing it right,*
> *or better.*
>
> JOHN UPDIKE

Whatever the outcome, the fact that you sought help is a major accomplishment.

What about God? Do you go to church? Temple? Meditate? Pray? Whatever connection you have with the Almighty, *you* had something to do with it. (If not, *everyone* would feel connected, and that's not the case.) Perhaps your accomplishments include abandoning one religious or spiritual path to find one closer to your heart.

Keep writing. The pump has been primed. This is a good point to set this book aside and spend some time writing and remembering. It will never be a complete list—the list of your achievements is nearly endless—but at some point, you'll approach the limit of your immediate memory. Pick up the book again and continue reading when the memories run out.

Now, read through your list. Note how much you have done, how much you have created—and how much more is available to you in the future.

Without regretting anything, imagine what you could have achieved if all these accomplishments had been pointed in a *single* direction—if all this creative energy had been directed toward fulfilling your heart's desire.

Again: no regrets. Don't look at the past and say, "What a waste." As Katherine Mansfield said, "Make it a rule of life never to regret and never to look back. Regret is an appalling waste of energy; you can't build on it; it's only good for wallowing in."

Use the energy to be *excited* about the future. If you're, say, thirty, don't think, "Thirty wasted years!" Most people don't begin making their own decisions until they're eighteen or twenty.

Let's arbitrarily say, "Life begins when you move out of your parents' house." (Although, for you it might be, "Life began when I got my first full-time job," or, if you're, say, Prince Charles and *never* plan to move out of your parents' house or get a job, "Life began when I got married" or "Life began when I got my divorce.")

For the first twenty-or-so years of life, we are in the hands of other people. If, then, you are thirty, and moved out when you were twenty, you really only have ten years of *your* life to consider.

> *Regret for time wasted*
> *can become*
> *a power for good*
> *in the time that remains,*
> *if we will only*
> *stop the waste*
> *and the idle,*
> *useless regretting.*
>
> ARTHUR BRISBANE

Look at what you've done in those years. Imagine how much you'll accomplish in the next similar period of time. This is something worth getting excited about.

The reward of a thing well done
is to have done it.

EMERSON

He is rich or poor
according to what he <u>is</u>,
not according to what he <u>has</u>.

Henry Ward Beecher

What Do You Have?

This list is a subset of the list you just made. It is a list of everything you're glad to have in your life *now*.

This is an exercise in recognizing what we often tend to take for granted. It is also an exercise in *gratitude*.

As you write this Inventory of Now, begin each item on the list with a phrase such as "I am grateful for . . ." or "I am thankful for . . ." or simply, "Thank you for . . ."

The list, then, will read,

> I am grateful for my health.
>
> I am grateful for my house.
>
> I am grateful for my relationship with . . .

and so on.

If you used 3x5 cards for the last exercise, you can go through those and pull out the ones that apply. Write at the top of each "I am grateful for" or, if the top is already taken, you can add to the bottom, "for which I am grateful."

If you didn't use 3x5 cards, go back over your list and copy the things you have now onto a new list. As you copy to the new list, preface each with "I am grateful for" or "I am thankful for."

Please do write "I am grateful for" before each thing on your list. Writing it once at the top of a page is not as effective—the physical writing of it, over and over, is important. And, if you're doing

> *In Hollywood*
> *all marriages are happy.*
> *It's trying to*
> *live together afterwards*
> *that causes the problems.*
>
> SHELLEY WINTERS

this process on a computer, for heaven sakes don't program it to add the phrase automatically!

(When I say "things," I mean anything—from people to cars to body parts to inner qualities to God. I don't mean to diminish any of them by calling them "things.")

After transferring all the things you have now from the list of your accomplishments, take a look at your current life. What did you leave out? What was so taken for granted you didn't include it on your list of achievements? What would you miss if it were taken from you? List those things, too.

What about your body? Even if some part of it doesn't look the way you'd like or function the way you want, what about the rest of it? Be grateful for those parts, and add them to your list.

How about your abilities? What do you know how to do that you're glad to know? Don't forget the skills you currently use to make money, the skills you *plan* to make money with, and the qualities that keep your friends coming back for more. (Review the list of qualities you made while working on your purpose.)

Speaking of friends, what about people? Who are the friends, lovers, acquaintances, spouses, children, relatives, coworkers, fellow-seekers you're glad to have in your life?

What about physical possessions? Look around. Your insurance agent may have recommended you make a list of this sort for years. Now's a good time to do it.

What about hobbies? Sports? The view from your window? The country, state, city, and neighborhood you live in? What freedoms do you have you'd hate to lose?

This is another of those lists that takes some time. It is, however, finite, and, with some time spent on it, can become fairly complete.

It is time well spent.

What do people want?
They want to be themselves,
they want to reach
their own potential.

Some of them want men,
some of them want women,
some of them want neither,
some of them want a pet turtle.

The bottom line is
self-expression.

PAUL KRASSNER

What Do You Want?

Here it is, the chapter you've been awaiting with eagerness, anxiety, or both. Here you'll discover what *you* want. You'll get to choose which of those wants you'll pursue, which you'll let pass, and which you'll postpone.

The underlying question of this chapter was best stated by Dr. Robert Schuller: "What would you attempt to do if you knew you could not fail?"

The answer to this question may require some reflection. I use the word *reflection* rather than *thought* because, as William James once said, "A great many people think they are thinking when they are merely rearranging their prejudices."

We all have prejudices. We think we don't know what we want, and that becomes a prejudice. We think we know *for sure* what we want, and that becomes a prejudice. We think we'll discover what we want sometime—but not now—and that becomes a prejudice.

To the degree you can, clear the slate. Start fresh. If a dream is truly your dream, it will survive the questions I am about to ask you. And if it is not your time to know, nothing I can ask will part the veil. You and your dream are safe. How well you learn about your dream in this process is entirely up to you.

If you happen to have some 3x5 cards lying around (ha!), get them. And a pen or pencil. If you're not using 3x5 cards, get three pads or piles of paper and make lists. Without 3x5 cards, you'll have to do a bit more recopying.

> *The great joy of the artist*
> *is to become aware*
> *of a higher order of things,*
> *to recognize by the compulsive*
> *and spontaneous manipulation*
> *of his own impulses*
> *the resemblance between human creation*
> *and what is called "divine" creation.*
>
> HENRY MILLER

Let's start by returning to the sanctuary.

Imagine going to the entryway. It opens. You step inside and bathe under the pure, white light just inside the entryway. You know that only that which is for your highest good can take place while you are in your sanctuary and during this process.

It's important to ask this for, as Cicero said, "the highest good." It's usual for various glamour-seeking parts of us to want something, not because *we* want it, but because it would be impressive to have. Obtaining these things only leads to woe. As St. Teresa of Avila said, "More tears are shed over answered prayers than unanswered ones." Or, to quote Oscar Wilde, "When the gods choose to punish us, they merely answer our prayers." Asking for the highest good of all concerned allows your true dreams to surface.

Go to the people mover and invite in your Master Teacher. See your Master Teacher appear through the white light of the people mover. Welcome your Master Teacher. Chat for a while about the process you are about to do.

This is a special process using your sanctuary. You can open your eyes, write things down, do things, and when you close your eyes again, you're immediately back in the sanctuary, precisely where you were when you opened your eyes. In fact, this entire process is done *in* the sanctuary—some of it with your eyes open, some with your eyes closed.

Open your eyes. You're about to make three piles of cards (or three lists). Each card will contain one item. As you write each item on a card, place the card in the appropriate pile.

Write a card to identify each pile. The first is labeled "WANTS," the second "QUALITIES and ABILITIES," and the third "LIMITATIONS."

Now, start filling out the cards. Free associate. A WANT ("Move to New York") might spark some of your QUALITIES and ABILITIES ("Adventurous," "Flexible," "Cultured"), and also some LIMITATIONS ("Not enough money," "Fear," "Leaving friends behind").

An ABILITY ("Talented") might prompt a WANT ("Become an opera singer"), which may inspire a LIMITATION ("Can't sing").

Once a card has been filled out on a given subject, it need not be repeated. One card containing the limitation "Fear," for example, is enough.

> *Live all you can;*
> *it's a mistake not to.*
> *It doesn't so much matter*
> *what you do in particular,*
> *so long as you have your life.*
> *If you haven't had that,*
> *what have you had?*
>
> HENRY JAMES

(Might as well fill that one out right now and get it over with.)

Don't bother sorting or prioritizing the cards. If you "want" a hot fudge sundae, write it down. And—even though your ultimate goals may be somewhat loftier—if money, fame, and power pop into your mind, by all means fill a card with them (three cards, in fact).

Tiny Tim, in listing his wants, said, "I'd love to see Christ come back to crush the spirit of hate and make men put down their guns. I'd also like just one more hit single." That's how our wants seem to go—some cosmic and grand; others personal and tiny.

In the process of decision-making and organization, putting it *all* down in writing, is known as a "data dump." Dump all the data onto cards, and the only sorting to be concerned about now is whether something is a WANT, a QUALITY and ABILITY, or a LIMITATION.

In writing all this down, remember that you're not committing to any of it. You'll have the opportunity to do that in a later chapter. For the purposes of this chapter, everything is just a "good idea."

And don't forget to have fun. Yes, it's your life you're looking at, and what you'll be doing with it, but that doesn't mean you have to be too *serious*. What we do to fill the time between our first cry and our last sigh is all a game, anyway. Treat this list with the same gravity you'd spend deciding what to do next Saturday afternoon. Shall we play football, baseball, or stage a ballet?

Take some time now and fill out the cards. If you run out of ideas, close your eyes and return to the sanctuary. Ask the Master Teacher for suggestions. Get all your WANTS, QUALITIES and ABILITIES, and LIMITATIONS on cards. Spend at least an hour doing this, although you may choose to take longer.

Do it 'til it's done, and return to this place in the book when your piles (or lists) are complete.

Excellent. Congratulations.

Now go through the cards (or lists) you made during the earlier process *What Is Your Purpose?* Write your purpose on a card and place it where you can easily see it. Does this remind you of other

> *All human activity*
> *is prompted by desire.*
>
> BERTRAND RUSSELL

WANTS, QUALITIES and ABILITIES, or LIMITA-TIONS? When you discovered your purpose, you made a list of qualities about yourself, and also actions you enjoyed. These can be added to the QUALITIES and ABILITIES or WANTS piles.

Now, look at the earlier listing of all the things you already have for which you are grateful. Add those things you want to include in your future to your WANTS list. Yes, you already have them, but *maintaining* them will probably take some time.

Almost *everything*—except perhaps that rock you brought back from Yosemite—requires *some* maintenance. To *maintain* what you currently have must be considered a goal for the future. So, add "Maintain house," "Maintain car," "Maintain relationship with

_____," etc. to your pile of WANTS. If any ABILITIES and QUALITIES or LIMITATIONS arise while adding these wants, make cards for them, too.

That done, let's turn to the WANT pile. Sort each want into one of five categories: Marriage/Family, Career/Professional, Social/Political, Religious/Spiritual, and Recreation/Fun.

I am making the assumption that *everyone* will want *some* recreation and/or fun in their lives regardless of which area of life they choose to primarily pursue. It seems to me that even the most serious devotee of a given path will want *some* recreation—in the sense of re-creation. So I'm making this a *parallel* category, one that can complement whatever major life area you choose to pursue.

In choosing the category (Marriage/Family, Career/Professional, Social/Political, Religious/Spiritual, or Recreation/Fun) in which to put each WANT, remember, "to thine own self be true." There may be an *obvious* category, but your personal *motivation* may make a particular WANT part of another category.

If one of your WANTS is, say, "Become a minister," is that because you want to be closer to God (Religious/Spiritual), you feel it would be a good platform from which to make social change (Social/Political), you think it would be a rewarding occupation (Career/Professional), or you want to intensify your relationship with someone who has a decided fondness for persons of the cloth (Marriage/Family)?

We must look closely at our motivations. As

> *It seems to me*
> *we can never give up*
> *longing and wishing*
> *while we are thoroughly alive.*
> *There are certain things we feel*
> *to be beautiful and good,*
> *and we must hunger after them.*
>
> GEORGE ELIOT

Madonna explained, "Losing my virginity was a career move."

You could, for example, put "Get married" under Career/Professional because everyone in the career you intend to pursue is properly espoused. Or, perhaps you're doing it for Religious/Spiritual reasons, following the dictate of Paul when he wrote, "It is better to marry than to burn" (I Corinthians, 7:9). You could be getting married for primarily societal reasons: "Any young man who is unmarried at the age of twenty-one," said Brigham Young, "is a menace to the community." Or, you might want to get married just because you want to get married (Marriage/Family).

There will be some overlapping, of course, but

put each WANT card in the category that *most* fits your motivation.

That done, review each of the Marriage/Family, Career/Professional, Social/Political, and Religious/Spiritual categories. (We'll look at Recreation/Fun a little later.)

Now, let's look ahead for the next, say, five years.

Take each category of wants separately, read them over, then close your eyes. Imagine what your life would be like in the next five years if you had a good number of those wants. Explore both the good *and* the bad, the up side and the down. Be neither too romantic nor too cynical. Take a look at it "straight on."

Use all the elements of your sanctuary to explore your life in that category. You can use the **people mover** to invite experts in the field and discuss the pros and cons; the **information retrieval system** to gather any facts or data you might find useful; the **video screen** to see yourself living that life. You can put on **ability suits** for each of the wants, and experience what that ability is like in the **ability suit practice area;** visit your **health center** and check on the health risks and advantages of each want; contemplate the category in your **sacred room;** and, of course, take your **Master Teacher** along with you throughout the whole process, discussing your reactions as you go.

And in all cases, ask yourself, "Would this direction in life fulfill my purpose?"

After spending time in your sanctuary with each of the four main areas of life, ask yourself, "During the next five years, within which *category* does my

> *Liberty,*
> *taking the word*
> *in its concrete sense,*
> *consists in*
> *the ability to choose.*
>
> SIMONE WEIL

heart's desire lie? During the next five years, which would give me the most satisfaction?"

If no answer is forthcoming, return with your Master Teacher to your sanctuary and explore. Is the choice between two? Examine them both, alternately. Which is most "on purpose"? Which category thrills your heart the most?

When you've chosen the category, go through all the wants within the category and select the one WANT you want the most. Again, use all the tools in the sanctuary to explore the pros and cons of each WANT, and choose the Big Want, the Big Goal, the Big Dream.

Why do I have you choose a category first, then a goal within that category? Usually, going for the

Big Goal within a category automatically fulfills many of the smaller goals within that category—not all, of course, but many. If you pick the *area* of life first, you will, by pursuing a Big Dream within that area, have more of what you want in the area of life you choose.

You are, of course, free to choose a Big Dream *outside* the area of life you are most drawn to. I have found, however, that most people tend to be more fulfilled by obtaining several goals within the area they prefer, rather than one big goal in an area they don't prefer as much. This is just an observation. Please make your choice of Big Dream yourself. Your Master Teacher will not steer you wrong.

One method of choosing between two Big Dreams that *seem* equally appealing is to make a list of all the pros and cons for each choice. As you read over these lists and compare them, one dream usually takes the lead.

Is this it? Is this your dream? The Big Dream? If yes, read on. If no, keep choosing.

Congratulations! But our work is not yet over.

When you have chosen, then *quantify* your dream. That is, make it a goal with *specific results* so that you'll know when you've achieved it.

This can be tough. People like to keep their dreams vague. "I want a family," is easier to say than, "I want a spouse, two children and a Rottweiler." But one is obtainable, one is not.

"I want a family" is not obtainable because the goal does not define what a family is. You could have a family of mice in your kitchen and your goal is fulfilled. "That's not what I mean." You could

> *As soon as man*
> *apprehends himself as free*
> *and wishes to use his freedom,*
> *his activity is play.*
>
> JEAN-PAUL SARTRE

have eighteen children and *still* not reach the goal, because some families have nineteen children. "That's not what I mean, either."

Then what *do* you mean?

Put something countable, something quantifiable in your goal so that you'll *know* when you've obtained it. You are not saddled with this goal forever and ever. When you reach it, you can choose a bigger one. For now, however, it's important to know what your goal is and be able to tell when you've reached it. (Remember: you haven't committed to anything yet.)

Here is where money often comes in. Although money is not a great goal *by itself,* as an indicator of whether or not you've obtained a goal, it can be excellent. As the people who understand money say, "Money is just a way of keeping score."

Rather than, "I am a singer," say "I am a singer making $50,000 (or $100,000, or $1,000,000) per year singing." Make the goal big enough to be a dream (if you're already making $40,000 at something, $42,000 is hardly a Big Dream), but small enough to be at least *partially* believable (if you're making nothing at something, jumping to $100,000,000 per year might be a bit too much for *any* of you to believe).

Some goals are quantifiable by time: "I am spending six months per year traveling." Others by amount: "I weigh 150 pounds." Others by degrees or recognition: "I have my medical license."

In setting a goal, it's fun to remember the movie *Bedazzled*. In a reworking of *Faust*, Peter Cook plays the devil and Dudley Moore—a short-order cook—sells his soul to be with a waitress who is indifferent to him. The devil catches the cook in one loophole after another. Moore wants to be married to his beloved, live in the country, and be rich. He gets his wish. *However*, she is in love with someone else. Moore asks for another chance. This time he wants to live in the country and have his beloved in love with him, too. The devil finds a loophole and makes them both nuns in a convent. And on it goes.

Be careful of the loopholes. If in doubt, add, ". . . for the highest good," to the end of your goal.

Write down your goal, your Big Dream.

Phrase your goal as though you already had it: "I am . . ." "I have . . . ." If your goal begins, "I want . . ." then your goal is *wanting*, not *being* or *having*.

> *Someday I want to be rich.*
> *Some people get so rich*
> *they lose all respect for humanity.*
> *That's how rich I want to be.*
>
> RITA RUDNER

Now, for a slight aside. Do you know how many minutes there are in a week? 10,080. That's 168 hours. That's your wealth in time. What you spend it on is your choice. No matter what you spend it on, however, you never get more than 10,080 minutes (168 hours) per week.

On a clean sheet of paper, or a new set of cards, write "168 Hours" at the top. Now, let's plan the next year.

Let's start with the basics. How many hours do you sleep each night? Multiply that times seven, and subtract that total from the week. If you sleep eight hours per night, eight hours times seven days is 56 hours per week of sleep. Subtract that from 168, and you have 112 hours remaining in the week.

Now, how many hours do you spend each day bathing, shaving, making up, dressing, and on other ablutions? One hour? Multiply that times seven and subtract from 112. That gives us 105 hours.

And now, eating. An hour a day? More? Less? Consider an average week and see how much time you spend preparing, consuming, and cleaning up after eating. Let's say it's an hour per day, or seven hours per week. That's seven from 105, which leaves us with 98 hours.

What about other necessary personal tasks? (Include things *only* if you *actually do them* on a *consistent* basis.) Cleaning (including car and laundry)? Shopping (including groceries)? Working out? Medical appointments or activities? Church? Meditation? And so on. Calculate how much time you spend per week on these (don't forget transportation to and from each), and subtract that from your total.

Let's say all that came to eighteen hours per week. That leaves you with eighty hours per week. *Half* the week spent maintaining the *basics*—and thus far we haven't even considered *work!*

We are, by the way, smack dab in the middle of something most people have a *very* difficult time facing: time. Yes, it's easy to accept the *concept* that there's "only so much time to go around," but, when faced with the reality—and the *limitation*—of time *in one's own life,* that's tough.

Facing your time limitation is, however, precisely what I'm asking you to do. It may be uncomfortable, but not as uncomfortable as looking back on this coming year after it has passed and saying, "I really *meant* to do that. Where did the time go?"

> *The real difference between men is energy.*
> *A strong will, a settled purpose,*
> *an invincible determination,*
> *can accomplish almost anything;*
> *and in this lies the distinction*
> *between great men and little men.*
>
> THOMAS FULLER

Now, go through the cards that list the things you already have and would like to maintain. Calculate how much time it would take each week to maintain each of them. Write that figure on the card. Do it for what you already have in *all* categories, but keep the cards within each category (the Marriage/Family cards in the Marriage/Family pile, etc.).

Some things may require zero maintenance (that rock from Yosemite). Others may need quite a lot (children, spouse, careers, major projects). Remember, these are the things you already *have*.

Don't forget to include those things that must be *paid for* to be maintained—mortgage or rent, car payments, etc. For those, calculate the number of hours you must work per week, at your current level of income, to pay for them. For example, if you make $10 per hour, and your car payment, gas, and maintenance is $320 per month, that's $80 per week, or eight hours per week to maintain the car.

Now the truly tough choices begin.

After all these hours are calculated, go through the cards of what you have and want to maintain, and compare each with the Big Dream you selected. For each item, ask yourself, "Which is more important?"

If what you want to maintain is more important, put that in one pile. Subtract the number of hours it takes to maintain this from the remaining hours in the week. If the Big Dream is more important, put the card of what you want to maintain back in the category pile it originally came from. For the Recreation/Fun category, you can set aside so many hours per week for various activities within the entire category. Subtract that from the hours remaining in the week.

Confused? Don't be surprised. These are difficult choices, and confusion, anger, fear, guilt, unworthiness, hurt feelings, discouragement, and all the other denizens of the comfort zone form a marching band when difficult choices present themselves. "You don't have to make these choices," they counsel, "They will make themselves," or "You need more information," or "Let's eat! We'll do this tomorrow."

I suggest, however, that you press on. Close your eyes. Take a deep breath. Get comfort and encouragement from your Master Teacher.

> *Our necessities are few*
> *but our wants are endless.*
>
> JOSH BILLINGS

Now calculate the cost for *basic necessities* (food, shelter, video rentals) not covered by the things you already have that you want to keep. How many hours each week will it take to make that much money? Subtract that number from your total.

How many hours do you have left? Is this enough to fulfill your Big Dream? If you don't have *at least* fourteen hours per week—two hours per day—to spend on your Big Dream, that may not be enough.

If your dream can really come true with *less* investment of time, it might be a rather small Big Dream.

Of course, you can set aside *more* than fourteen hours for your Big Dream. The more time you spend, the more quickly your Dream will come true.

Now comes the fun part. Take your Big Dream, and see how many WANTS would *automatically* (or almost automatically) be fulfilled by achieving the Big Dream. For example, if your Big Dream was to become a movie star, the smaller wants of "Live in Los Angeles," "Be famous," "Make $1,000,000," and "Meet Brooke Shields," would naturally follow. If you fulfilled the Big Dream, a great many of the smaller dreams would almost effortlessly come to pass.

It's okay to go into *any* of the piles and pull out dreams that fit within the Big Dream. But be honest, now, because with enough bending and twisting, almost *any* goal can fit behind a big enough dream. "I want to be an airline pilot, so watching every movie that comes out will better help me tell the passengers what the movie is about on board the plane," or "I want to write a novel about being rich, so I think I'll take all my money and buy a Rolls Royce so I can get in the mood."

Now, back to the tough part. *Eliminate* all wants that are in *direct opposition* to your Big Dream. "Live in New York City" and "Experience the joys of small town life" do not belong in the same dream. One of them must go.

Be ruthless. "Oh, I can stay in Kansas and become a movie star." Uh-huh.

Please remember that simultaneously pursuing Big Dreams from two different categories is difficult. If, for example, your main area of activity is *not* Marriage/Family, please keep this in mind: if the romantic relationship you may seek *in addition to* your Big Dream does not provide you with *more time* to

> *Men are my hobby;*
> *if I ever got married*
> *I'd have to give it up.*
>
> MAE WEST

pursue your dream, either your Big Dream or the relationship will suffer. Usually both. I don't like this harsh reality any more than you do. It seems, however, to be the way it is.

If you still have time in your week (which is doubtful), you can add other wants to your week *providing* they are not in opposition to your Big Dream. The smart thing is to choose additional goals that somehow support or enhance the Big Dream—but as soon as you run out of hours, stop. That's it.

You can now combine the piles of The Big Dream And All That Comes With It and the pile of things already in your life you chose to maintain. Review your choices. Behold: your next year (and probably beyond).

Write at the top of each card in the new pile the following: "I am . . ." or "I have . . . ." No longer are these mere wants. They are goals.

Hold on to the WANTS *not* in the "I am . . ." or "I have . . ." pile. We'll get to them in the next chapter.

For now, review the LIMITATIONS pile. For each limitation, ask yourself how you can turn it into an *advantage*. How can it become an *ally* in fulfilling your Big Dream? We've already looked at fear becoming the energy to do your best in a new situation, guilt as the energy for personal change, unworthiness as a way of keeping on track, hurt feelings as a way of remembering the caring, anger as the energy for change, and discouragement as a reminder of our courage.

See if you can find a *positive use* for everything on your list. Impatience? Be impatient for success. Stubborn? Let it become determination. Big ego? Bravo! Put it behind your goal. Laziness? Become lazy about doing the things *not* on the way to fulfilling your Dream. Procrastinate about procrastination. And so on.

Write the positive attribute for each former limitation in larger letters on the same card. Any time you feel this limitation coming on, you can return to the card and see what the positive use for that former limitation might be. Remember: it's all *your* energy. Align it toward your goal. Be creative. If some limitations seemingly can't be turned into assets, set them aside for now.

Turn now to the QUALITIES and ABILITIES pile. Review each quality and ability. Imagine how each quality and ability can be used to fulfill your Big Dream.

> *Neither a lofty degree of intelligence*
> *nor imagination*
> *nor both together*
> *go to the making of genius.*
> *Love, love, love,*
> *that is the soul of genius.*
>
> WOLFGANG AMADEUS MOZART

Look again at the LIMITATIONS for which you have not yet seen a positive use. What QUALITIES and ABILITIES would best help you in overcoming each limitation? Let the qualities and abilities gang up—let their deck be stacked in your favor; it is, after all, *your* deck.

Review again the cards in the "I am . . ." and "I have . . ." pile—your Big Dream and its companions. Compare each dream in that pile with your purpose. See how each fulfills your purpose perfectly.

Close your eyes, find yourself in your sanctuary, thank your Master Teacher, watch the Master Teacher disappear into the white light of the people mover. As you turn to go, you notice some writing on the wall of your sanctuary—your Big Dream.

Read it, enjoy it, become it. Move to the white light of your entryway. Bathe in it, breathe it in. Leave your sanctuary, and return to the outside world to make your Dream come true.

*The secret of contentment
is knowing how
to enjoy what you have,
and to be able to lose
all desire
for things beyond your reach.*

LIN YUTANG

Completion

You've discovered and chosen your Big Dream, your Heart's Desire. What? No cheering? No celebration?

Not quite yet.

Lying "in the ruins" are all those other heart's desires—all those deserted little 3x5 cards. The reminders of the dreams that won't immediately—and might never—come true.

Sigh.

Welcome to success.

Remember that the sadness you feel is a reminder of your caring, and the caring is *your* caring—available to place behind the Big Dream *you* have chosen to pursue.

It is important to complete each WANT that you will not—for now—be pursuing. "Complete" doesn't mean do it; complete means declare your involvement with it, for now, done. "Complete" doesn't mean to physically finish; "complete" means *you* are complete with it—that you have completed all you're going to do about it, for now.

The down side is that you must say good-bye to some valuable and desirable dreams—perhaps for good. (When we say good-bye, we never really know for how long it's going to be.)

The up side is that declaring things complete frees the mental, emotional, and physical energy we've been holding in reserve for the achievement of that goal.

This can be a significant amount of energy.

> *I shun father and mother*
> *and wife and brother*
> *when my genius calls me.*
>
> EMERSON

For each WANT that didn't make the "I am . . ." or "I have . . ." pile and for each thing you currently have that you chose not to maintain, read it, consider it, and say, out loud, "This is complete for now." Say good-bye to it, and place it face down. Pick up another card and repeat the process.

Take your time. You may feel the sadness, or you may feel the freeing of energy. You may cry and laugh at the same time. Always have your Big Dream clearly in mind, so that you can direct the newly freed energy toward it.

With some cards you may feel that, after all, you *can* achieve this smaller dream, too. You'll just sleep less at night, or something. This is the newly freed energy (or perhaps the comfort zone) talking. Stick to your plan. Declare the smaller dream complete. Direct the energy toward the Big Dream and move on.

If the dreams you are completing involve other people, let them know you will not be doing anything more about these dreams. This is only fair. The most important person to tell, however, is yourself.

Sometimes the "extra energy" is stored in material value. If you choose not to maintain certain physical posessions, sell them. Or donate them. Use that good will toward your Dream. Don't wait for the things you're not maintaining to rot. Cash them in. Convert them into energy and channel that energy toward your Dream.

The amount of power freed by telling yourself you no longer choose to put energy into something can be remarkable. Be prepared for extra energy. Be prepared, as well, to channel that newly liberated energy toward your Dream.

The way to begin that is through *commitment*.

Want to be a composer?

If you can <u>think design</u>,
you can <u>execute design</u>—
it's only a bunch of air molecules,
who's gonna check up on you?
Just follow these simple instructions:

1. Declare your <u>intention</u>
to create a "composition."

2. <u>Start</u> a piece at <u>some time</u>.

3. Cause <u>something to happen</u>
<u>over a period of time</u>
(it doesn't matter what happens
in your "time hole"—
we have critics to tell us
whether it's any good or not,
so we won't worry about that part).

4. <u>End the piece at some time</u>
(or keep it going, telling the audience
it is a "work in progress").

5. Get a part-time job so you can
continue to do stuff like this.

FRANK ZAPPA

Committing to Your Dream —and Keeping That Commitment

Perhaps you've noticed that I haven't yet asked you to commit to your Dream. This is because, when we commit to something, *and we really mean it,* the manure hits the fan and the fan is running.

Before asking you to commit, I wanted you to understand this process, and offer some suggestions on how to use the manure as fertilizer.

Most people don't know about this process, because most people don't keep most of their agreements.

Most people add a silent, unconscious modifying phrase to all their commitments: ". . . as long as it's not uncomfortable."

What most people don't realize is that discomfort is one of the *values* of commitments, one of the reasons for making a commitment in the first place.

Within us is an automatic goal-fulfillment mechanism. When we commit to something, we are telling the goal-fulfillment mechanism, "I want this." The goal-fulfillment mechanism says, "Fine. I'll arrange for that." And it does, by performing various functions—individually or collectively:

- It looks to see what lessons we must learn in order to have our goal; then it arranges for those lessons. Sometimes, these lessons come in pleasant ways (we notice an article on what

> *For anything worth having*
> *one must pay the price;*
> *and the price is always*
> *work, patience, love, self-sacrifice.*
>
> JOHN BURROUGHS

we need to know in a magazine; a conversation with a friend reveals information to us; a song on the radio has a line that tells us something important). At other times, the lessons are unpleasant (someone we must listen to—a boss, for example—tells us "in no uncertain terms" what we need to know; or we get sick, and the doctor tells us what we need to do "or else").

- The goal-fulfillment mechanism sees what stands in the way of our having what we want and removes it. Again, sometimes this can be pleasant (if the goal is a new car, someone offers us a great price for our old car), or unpleasant (our car is stolen, totaled, or breaks down).

There is something else the goal-fulfillment mechanism does: it gives us numerous opportunities to expand our comfort zone.

In order to have something new, we must expand our comfort zone to include the new thing. The bigger the new thing, the more the comfort zone must expand. And *comfort zones are most often expanded through discomfort*. As they say in weight training: "No pain; no gain."

Lifting weights seems like a terrible waste of time, a lot of work, and unnecessary pain, but lifting weights makes you strong enough to fulfill the goals you *do* want to achieve. The same is true with expanding the comfort zone.

When people don't understand that being uncomfortable is part of the process of achievement, they use the discomfort as a reason not to do. Then they don't get what they want. We must learn to tolerate discomfort in order to grow.

This process of growth is known as "grist for the mill." When making flour in an old stone mill, it is necessary to add gravel to the wheat before grinding it. This gravel is known as *grist*. The small stones that make up the grist rub against the grain as the mill wheel passes over them. The friction causes the wheat to be ground into a fine powder. If it weren't for the grist, the wheat would only be crushed. To grind wheat fine enough for flour requires grist. After the grinding, the grist is sifted out, and only the flour remains.

> *The expectations of life*
> *depend upon diligence;*
> *the mechanic that would*
> *perfect his work*
> *must first sharpen his tools.*
>
> CONFUCIUS

When we commit to something, the automatic goal-fulfillment mechanism throws grist in our mill. It's all designed to give us our goal.

If we don't understand the process, however, we protest, "Why are you throwing gravel in with my wheat? Stop that!" The dutiful miller uses no grist, and we wind up with crushed wheat. "This isn't what I wanted. I wanted *flour.*"

When we order flour, we must be prepared for grist in our mill. We must become an "eager learner." *Whatever* comes along, look for the lesson. *Assume* it's for your good, no matter how bad it seems.

No, there's no need to run out and *invite* disaster, just as one doesn't have to bring gravel to the mill. The necessary experiences will take place. Our job is not to *seek* them, but to take part in and learn from the ones that are presented to us.

Maxwell Maltz explains the process this way:

> Your automatic creative mechanism oper-ates in terms of goals and end results. Once you give it a definite goal to achieve, you can depend on its automatic guidance system to take you to that goal much bet-ter than "You" ever could by conscious thought. "You" supply the goal by think-ing in terms of end results. Your automat-ic mechanism then supplies the means whereby.

How do we know when there's grist in our mill? When we feel the comfort zone acting up, there's grist in the mill. If we discard the grist (that is, honor the comfort zone's dictates), we have crushed wheat. If we use the grist to gain strength and learn the lesson at hand (that is, continue on our commit-ted course despite the protestations of the comfort zone), we have flour.

Keeping agreements with others is, of course, an excellent method for getting what we want from them. If we keep our agreements, people learn to trust us. If we break our agreements, they don't. It's hard to imagine people giving something of sub-stance to someone they don't trust.

People may say, "Oh, that's all right," when we make our apologies, but it is seldom truly all right with people. "Unfaithfulness in keeping an ap-pointment is an act of clear dishonesty," Horace Mann explained 150 years ago. "You may as well

> *I could never think well of
> a man's intellectual or moral character,
> if he was habitually unfaithful
> to his appointments.*
>
> NATHANIEL EMMONS

borrow a person's money as his time."

Although keeping agreements is a good technique for building trust with others, the more important reason for keeping agreements is building trust with *ourselves*.

If we frequently break agreements—either with others or with ourselves—we are training ourselves to ignore our own word. Committing to something, then, means nothing. Committing to a Big Dream is about as significant as saying we will learn to fly—sounds nice, it would be fun, but it's not going to happen.

Committing to a dream is not a one-time occurrence. It must be done daily, hourly, continually. We must *choose* to commit to our *choice,* over and over.

The test of this commitment is *action*. If I say, "I commit to being a great dancer," and then don't practice, that's not a commitment; that's not dance; it's just talk. Conversely, if I'm practicing dance, I don't need to tell myself how committed I am. My action *is* my demonstrated commitment.

When we commit and act, we are confronted by the comfort zone. We are tempted to stop, encouraged to stop, *demanded* to stop. If we move ahead anyway—we expand the comfort zone, learn a necessary lesson, and the commitment becomes stronger. That causes us to come up against the comfort zone again, and the process continues.

Here are some suggestions for making and keeping commitments:

1. Don't make commitments you don't plan to keep. Some people are so casual about making agreements: "Talk to you tomorrow," "Let's get together next week," and, one of my favorites, "I'll have him call you back." (You *will?* What if he doesn't want to call me back?)

Most people like to pretend that these "casual" commitments don't count. They do. Every time we give our word, it counts. For the most part, people give their word entirely too often. Our word is a precious commodity and should be treated as such.

Imagine a commitment as a precious jewel. When you give it to someone, the other person has the jewel. When you keep the commitment, the jewel is returned to you. If you fail to keep the agreement, however, the jewel is gone forever. (This is true of agreements with yourself as well.)

If we remember this jewel analogy each time

> *You will never "find" time*
> *for anything.*
> *If you want time*
> *you must make it.*

CHARLES BUXTON

we give our word, we tend to be more careful. Our word *is* a precious jewel; each time we give it, we risk losing it. Don't take that risk unless you plan to "cover your assets."

2. Learn to say no. When we commit to a Dream, one of the great tests of our sincerity is whether we say no to things not on the way to that Dream. If we commit to moving to another city, for example, temptations from the city we have not yet left appear: we're given a raise and a promotion; we hear about a larger, better, less-expensive apartment; a 24-hour gourmet restaurant (that delivers) opens nearby; and we meet Someone Wonderful.

If we're *really* committed to moving, to all of these we must say, "No." Talk about the comfort zone acting up! Wait until Someone Wonderful calls and invites you out (or, worse, *in*) on the same evening you planned to go over street maps of the city you plan to move to. Ouch.

Beyond this, we are programmed not to say no to people we know. Conversely, we are also programmed to automatically "no" all strangers. This dual programming makes for a small circle of the same friends with whom we do things we don't necessarily like. To pursue a Big Dream, we must learn to say no to both programmings.

3. Make conditional agreements. Doctors learn to say, "I'll be there, unless I get a call from the hospital." You can, too. If there is *potentially* something more important than the agreement you are about to make, let the other person know. "I'd love to have lunch, unless I get a call-back on my audition," "I can make it, unless Greenpeace calls," or "Yes, I'll do it, if I can find a sitter for the kids." Do not, however, use this as a substitute for saying no. That turns your Big Dream into a Big Excuse and robs it of some power. Use the condition *only* with agreements you want to—and plan to—keep.

4. Keep the commitments you make. As an exercise, practice keeping *all* agreements you make—no matter how difficult, no matter how costly. This will do two things: first, it will build strength, character, and inner trust. Second, it will get you to reread suggestions #1, #2, and #3 and follow them more carefully.

5. Write commitments down. Keep a calendar and write agreements down—*including agreements you make with yourself.* Don't just say, "I'm exercising

> *To accomplish our destiny*
> *it is not enough*
> *merely to guard prudently*
> *against road accidents.*
> *We must also*
> *cover before nightfall*
> *the distance assigned*
> *to each of us.*
>
> ALEXIS CARREL

tomorrow morning," write it down. Set a time. Arrange for it. Make it as important as an agreement you made with someone else—a *very important* someone else.

You might want to write on a sheet of paper, "All agreements with myself shall be in writing. Everything else is just a good idea." Then place the paper somewhere you will read it—often. Write it on every page in your calendar. Eventually, there will be a difference between commitments you make with yourself and those things that would be nice, would be beneficial, but are not going to happen.

6. Renegotiate at the earliest opportunity. As soon as a possible conflict arises, contact the person with whom you have the first agreement. Unless the original agreement was conditional, the *way* in which you renegotiate an agreement is important.

"Something more important than my agreement with you has come up," is not the best way. It's a form of breaking the agreement, just in advance. "I know I have an agreement with you, and I still plan to keep it, but something important has come up, and I wonder if we might be able to reschedule." That asks permission. If granted, you get a second chance at reclaiming your jewel. If *not* granted, see #4.

And now you are ready to commit to your goal—your Dream.

It's important to commit to the fulfillment of the goal, not just to a certain amount of time spent pursuing the goal. Some people's commitments sound like this: "I'll spend two years pursuing this goal, and see what happens."

When we commit to *pursuing,* our goal is then *pursuing,* and we will pursue. We won't necessarily *get* what we're pursuing, because getting it is not our goal—pursuing it is.

It is fine, however, to add a time statement to your dream. "By <u>DATE</u> I am . . ." or "By <u>DATE</u> I have . . . ."

This makes it a bigger challenge, of course. We will know precisely when we have succeeded in fulfilling our Dream, because we put specific parameters on the goal (so much money, a certain creden-

> *Everyone is necessarily
> the hero of his own life story.*
>
> JOHN BARTH

tial, etc.). Adding time to our goal lets us know precisely when we have *failed,* too.

This is important. To say we want something by a certain date shows us what we must do *today, right now,* to make that happen. It gets us going. If we don't achieve it, it gives us a chance to look back, see what must be done differently in the future, correct our course, set a new date, recommit, and continue on.

So, add a time to your dream, and, if you so choose, commit.

The time to commit is now.

And now. And now. And now. And now . . .

When you feel in your gut
what you are
and then dynamically pursue it
—don't back down
and don't give up—
then you're going to
mystify a lot of folks.

BOB DYLAN

*Keep away from people
who try to belittle
your ambitions.
Small people
always do that,
but the really great
make you feel that you, too,
can become great.*

MARK TWAIN

Keep Your Goals
Away from the Trolls

There is a type of crab that cannot be caught—it is agile and clever enough to get out of any crab trap. And yet, these crabs are caught by the thousands every day, thanks to a particularly human trait they possess.

The trap is a wire cage with a hole at the top. Bait is placed in the cage, and the cage is lowered into the water. One crab comes along, enters the cage, and begins munching on the bait. A second crab joins him. A third. Crab Thanksgiving. Yumm. Eventually, however, all the bait is gone.

The crabs could easily climb up the side of the cage and through the hole, but they do not. They stay in the cage. Other crabs come along and join them—long after the bait is gone. And more.

Should one of the crabs realize there is no further reason to stay in the trap and attempt to leave, the other crabs will gang up on him and stop him. They will repeatedly pull him off the side of the cage. If he is persistent, the others will tear off his claws to keep him from climbing. If he persists still, they will kill him.

The crabs—by force of the majority—stay together in the cage. The cage is hauled up, and it's dinnertime on the pier.

The chief difference between these crabs and humans is that these crabs live under water and humans don't.

> *Commonplace minds*
> *usually condemn*
> *what is beyond the reach*
> *of their understanding.*
>
> FRANÇOIS DE LA ROCHEFOUCAULD

Anyone who has a dream—one that might get him out of what he perceives to be a trap—had best beware of the fellow-inhabitants of the trap.

The human crabs (I call them trolls) do not usually use physical force—although they're certainly not above it. They generally don't need it. They have more effective methods at hand, and in mouth—innuendo, doubt, ridicule, derision, mockery, sarcasm, scorn, sneering, belittlement, humiliation, jeering, taunting, teasing, lying, and several dozen others.

The way to handle such people is the same method used by Jonathan Joffrey Crab on *his* clan. (Remember that book about the crab who wasn't content to walk around; he wanted to learn underwater ballet?) Jonathan, knowing the dangers of attempted departure from the cage, said, "Hey! This is fun! What a gathering of crabs! I'm going to go get some more!" And he danced off to freedom.

My suggestion: keep your goals away from the trolls.

People don't like to see others pursuing their dreams—it reminds them how far from living their own dreams they are. In talking you out of your dreams, they are talking themselves back into their comfort zone. They will give you every rational lie they ever gave themselves—and add a few more. If you don't believe the lies with the same degree of devotion the trolls do, get ready for Big Time Disapproval.

Why bother? Consider your Dream a fragile seed. It's small now. It needs protection and lots of nurturing. Eventually, it will be strong—stronger than the slings and arrows of outrageously limited people.

When you've obtained your goal, *then* tell them about it. Even though faced with irrefutable evidence, the most common expression you'll hear will be, "I don't believe it!" If they can't believe reality, imagine how much difficulty they'd have believing in your Dream.

This warning, of course, does not apply to close friends and supporters who have always believed in you and offer only encouragement. If you're not sure whether to discuss your dream with someone, talk about a "friend" who has a similar Dream. If the response is positive, you're in good hands. If the response is, "What a silly thing to do," it would be a

> *To keep your secret*
> *is wisdom;*
> *but to expect others*
> *to keep it*
> *is folly.*
>
> SAMUEL JOHNSON

silly thing, indeed, to share your goals with this person.

If some people should hear of your Dream and start telling you all the reasons why you can't possibly do it, you can (a) walk away, or (b) listen to them with compassion as they describe the parameters of their own comfort zones—the limitations that may keep them firmly in the trap until it is hauled up.

The world doesn't want
to hear about
the labor pains.
It only wants
to see the baby.

JOHNNY SAIN

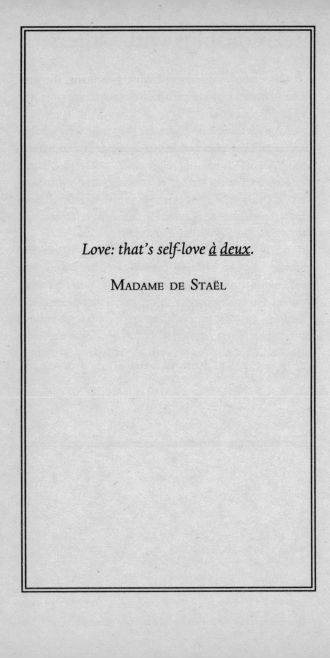

Love: that's self-love à deux.

MADAME DE STAËL

Relationships with Others

Once you've discovered what you want, the purpose of relationships becomes clear—to support and celebrate that goal.

Like dividing our desire for romance into smaller desires, we can also divide our desire for relationships into specific kinds of relationships. These include friendships, contractual relationships, companionship, mutual-goal relationships, power-point relationships, romantic relationships, service relationships, and marriage. I'll devote a chapter to each.

Knowing the kinds of relationships available and the kind you're looking for will not only help you find the relationships you want, but help define what you have to offer others in return. This makes for a "cleaner" relationship, with fewer misunderstandings about what each party expects to get from the relationship, which helps everyone involved avoid working at cross-purposes.

Dear,
never forget
one little point:

It's my business.

You just work here.

ELIZABETH ARDEN
TO HER HUSBAND

Contractual Relationships

Contractual relationships are the fundamental relationships between human beings. They are the you-do-this-for-me-and-I'll-do-this-for-you relationships.

Sometimes the same service is exchanged ("You scratch my back; I'll scratch yours"). In other contracts, the medium of exchange is different ("You give me an ice cream cone; I'll give you some money").

As we've explored, any society that rises above the law of the jungle includes the fundamental contract: "I won't physically harm your person or property as long as you don't physically harm mine."

Some contractual relationships are complete in and of themselves—buying the ice cream cone, for example. In other relationships (which we will be discussing soon), a contract is formed in addition to, or as a part of, a larger goal. If, for example, people choose to be friends, they may make any number of contracts to support that goal ("Meet you in front of the movie theater at seven," "Call you tomorrow," and so on).

Almost every relationship, then, includes contracts—either stated or implied. This being the case, allow me to narrow the definition of contractual relationships to include only those which are exclusively contractual—buying an ice cream cone, getting your teeth filled, renting an apartment. If you form a more elaborate relationship with the ice cream seller, dentist, or landlord, then it is no longer an exclusively contractual relationship.

> *Even in the common affairs of life,*
> *in love, friendship, and marriage,*
> *how little security have we*
> *when we trust our happiness*
> *in the hands of others!*

WILLIAM HAZLITT
1822

Contractual relationships can, of course, be friendly without people becoming friends. We often see friendly contractual relationships among co-workers, neighbors, in business—even relatives.

The satisfaction you get from fulfilling contractual relationships with integrity, pride, and friendliness can enhance your loving relationship with yourself.

"What Ho!" I said,

"What Ho!" said Motty.

"What Ho! What Ho!"

"What Ho! What Ho! What Ho!"

*After that it seemed rather difficult
to go on with the conversation.*

P. G. WODEHOUSE

*True happiness is
of a retired nature,
and an enemy
to pomp and noise;
it arises,
in the first place,
from the enjoyment
of one's self;
and,
in the next,
from the friendship
and conversation
of a few
select companions.*

JOSEPH ADDISON
1711

Friendships

Friends are people we spend time with because we like spending time with them. They're the people we save our anecdotes for, watch the game with, gossip with (and about).

People we see only occasionally, we tend to think of as acquaintances (but to their faces they're our fast friends). Friends we spend a great deal of time with, or like better than our other friends, we call best friends.

That seems to be the basis of friendship—liking: we like being with them, like the way they treat us, and simply like them. This eventually leads to love.

Unlike romantic relationships, in which lust becomes love in a dangerously brief time, liking turning to loving in friendships is an unhurried, gradual, organic process.

Because of the freedom and enjoyment friends give each other, friendships are among the most valuable relationships around.

The danger of friendships: having so many of them that they detract or take time away from pursuing your Big Dream.

Once the realization is accepted
that even between
the <u>closest</u> human beings
infinite distances continue to exist,
a wonderful living side by side
can grow up,
if they succeed in
loving the distance between them
which makes it possible
for each to see the other
whole against the sky.

RAINER MARIA RILKE

Companionship

Companionship implies not just friendship, but spending time together in which visiting with the other person is not the central reason for being together.

Whereas friends get together to have dinner so they can discuss "what's new," companions eat together because they enjoy sharing a meal in each other's company. Sometimes companions share hardly a word during dinner. When asked why they didn't say anything, companions often respond, "I didn't have anything to say," or "We don't have to talk; we just like being together."

People for whom talking is a Main Event of relating—people who talk during sex, whisper to each other during plays, and take small bites of dinner so they are only one brief swallow away from their next spectacular comment—often have trouble understanding companionship. If you're not going to talk, or do something together you can talk about immediately afterwards, what's the point in being together? Companions, on the other hand, don't understand why the more verbal variety of friends are always *talking* so much.

The relative health of a companion relationship can best be determined by that mercurial standard—*motivation*. Is the motivation for being together to avoid loneliness, or because you enjoy being together? The latter, obviously, tends to be the healthier relationship.

Companionship is probably one of the best

> RICK: *I mean, what AM*
> *I supposed to call you?*
> *My "Girl Friend"?*
> *My "Companion"?*
> *My "Roommate"?*
> *Nothing sounds quite right!*
>
> JOANIE: *How about your*
> *"Reason for Living"?*
>
> RICK: *No, no, I need something*
> *I can use around the office.*
>
> GARRY TRUDEAU
> "DOONESBURY"

reasons for getting married, living together, or becoming roommates. This is especially true if the partners grow into it, rather than jump into it. If you are naturally and gradually spending more and more time together, and you both consider the time well spent, living together (not necessarily sexually, of course, but not necessarily not) is a reasonable option.

Before making this move, however (one that has turned otherwise good companions into best of enemies), you might want to pass the Living Together Test suggested by Melba Colgrove, Ph.D.— drive together across country and back. These ten-to-fifteen days of sharing the psychologically enclosed space of a car and motel rooms (unless you intend to have separate bedrooms and bathrooms in your living arrangement), eating together, and sharing such responsibilities as driving, navigating, choosing destinations, and negotiating sightseeing, will separate true companions from those who should stay friends-who-hang-out-together-a-lot.

The term *longtime companion* has taken on a special meaning in the last few years. It's used by gays to describe their significant others.

Inexplicably, gays are not permitted to honor their committed relationships with marriage—at least not in a ceremony recognized by law. Primarily as a result of the AIDS crisis, gays wanted a way of referring to their significant other, but in a term less sexually charged than *lover* and more accurate than *good friend* or *roommate. Longtime companion,* or simply *companion* (especially since the *New York Times* and other major newspapers have *finally* allowed the term in their obituary sections), seems to be filling the need.

This use of the term *companionship,* however, would be what I'm referring to as *marriage* in this book.

*If you don't do it
excellently,
don't do it at all.*

*Because if it's not excellent,
it won't be profitable or fun,
and if you're not in business
for fun or profit,
what the hell
are you doing there?*

ROBERT TOWNSEND

Mutual-Goal Relationships

When people come together because they are pursuing the same goal—whether it be social, political, financial, creative, sexual,* spiritual, or any other goal which can be pursued by more than one person—it's a mutual-goal relationship.

Sometimes we choose to be in these relationships (two or more actors getting together to practice and pursue acting), and sometimes we are placed in them (being put on the same project with others at work). As friendly and supportive as these relations might be, the primary reason for their existence is the common goal.

Once the goal is achieved, these relationships tend to end. When two or more people find the relationship particularly satisfying, they may (if dumb) sabotage the goal so the relationship continues, or (if smart) choose a new goal.

---

*Yes, this is the kind of relationship people form when they want to fulfill the mutual goal of sexual gratification without having a romance. A skip-the-candy-bring-the-condoms kind of relationship. (I put in that last sentence not to be vulgar or to endorse promiscuity, but to subtly encourage safe-sex.)

I love Mickey Mouse
more than any woman
I've ever known.

WALT DISNEY

Power-Point Relationships

Power-point relationships are a form of mutual-goal relationships, but differ in that the power generated in the relationship is fed to one person. This person becomes the *power-point* and uses the power to achieve a goal benefiting the entire group.

The power fed to the person acting as the power-point can be in the form of information, money, professional support services, sex, housing, food, transportation, training, or any other valuable commodity.

A classic example of the power-point relationship is an athlete training for an Olympic event. The athlete takes the power from a trainer, coach, nutritionist, masseur, corporate sponsor, and many others, and focuses that energy on training for the event. When the athlete wins, *all* the members of the power-point team win.

Power-point relationships are often seen in the creative arts when, for example, an actor will have a writer, director, make-up artist, drama coach, cinematographer, and many others working "behind the scenes" to make the actor's performance the best possible. Anytime people work behind the scenes supporting one person, or a small group of people, that's a power-point relationship.

In one-on-one relationships, one person can feed power to the other, as long as it is clearly understood that all gains made by the power-point person are mutual.

If partner A pursues a career goal while partner

> *I have sacrificed
> everything in my life
> that I consider precious
> in order to advance
> the political career
> of my husband.*
>
> PAT NIXON

B supplies a supportive home environment, encouragement, nurturing, and also supplies person A with the invaluable commodities of time and peace of mind (and a Pentium 90), person B is fully entitled to share in person A's success. If person B expects nothing in return, then it's a *service* relationship (described shortly).

This is the genesis of the phrase, "behind every great man is a great woman"—although it could certainly be the man behind the woman, the woman behind the woman, or the man behind the man.

For power-point relationships to work, all parties must clearly know and agree that they are in a power-point relationship. This prevents the power-point from feeling he or she is exploiting the others, and prevents the others from feeling exploited.

The point person in a power-point relationship is like the point of an arrow—essential, but useless without the shaft, feathers, string, and bow.

Although it may appear the point does all the "work," an arrow piercing its target is a result of teamwork. If any member of the team were missing, it would be difficult, if not impossible, to achieve the same goal.

What a recreation it is to be in love!

It sets the heart aching so delicately,
there's no taking a wink of sleep
for the pleasure of the pain.

GEORGE COLMAN THE YOUNGER
1762–1836

Romantic Relationships

Although I certainly have done my share of criticizing the illusion of romantic relationships, they can, and do, have their place. I tend to challenge, however, their place as the basis for marriage or their existence as a prerequisite to a satisfying life.

But a romantic relationship for its own sake—that is, consciously seeking what's available in and from a romantic relationship—is fine.

What do romantic relationships contain? Passion, lust, fulfillment, physical merging, and a sense of "Eureka! I've found it! No, this time *for real! I mean it!*"

Is there illusion in romantic relationship? You betcha. There is also illusion in a movie, watching TV, reading a book, or listening to music. As long as we accept it's an illusion, we can lose ourselves in it and have a great time.

My criticism of romantic love is that people confuse the illusion with the reality—it's as though a group of people thought the food on television was real, and were then disappointed each time they reached for it, only to bruise their hands on the unforgiving hardness of the TV screen. These people—who believe that their television sets are actually filled with Big Macs, Bud Lights, and Chee-tos ready for them to eat *if they could only figure out how to get them outta there*—might stay in their living room and starve to death.

To this hungry crew, I come along and say, "The food is in the kitchen!" Those who've already determined that television may be the source of entertain-

> *Husbands think we should know*
> *where everything is—*
> *like the uterus*
> *is a tracking device.*
>
> *He asks me,*
> *"Roseanne, do we have any Chee-tos left?"*
>
> *Like he can't*
> *go over to that sofa cushion*
> *and lift it himself.*
>
> ROSEANNE

ment but not physical nourishment, welcome my news. Others, who still believe the BLT is in the TV, will find my suggestion (that there is nothing in the television but electrons) intrusive and rude—as though I were trying to deprive them of the BLT they rightfully deserved.

Granted, if someone sits next to you during a particularly dramatic, touching, funny, or exciting television moment and says, "Those aren't people; they're actors," "That's not a real space ship; that's just a movie set," or "His head didn't really explode; that's just special effects," the truth-teller might be understandably barred from the TV room.

I hope I haven't been so enthusiastically debunking of romantic love that I seem to be a pest. If I have, please forgive me. The illusion that romantic love is real, and all other reality less real, is a powerful one. Once you know, however, that romantic love is an illusion, well, then, *¡viva la ilusión! ¡viva el románico!*

*It's curious how,
when you're in love,
you yearn to go about
doing acts of kindness
to everybody.*

*I am bursting
with a sort of
yeasty benevolence
these days,
like one of those
chaps in Dickens.*

P. G. WODEHOUSE

Service Relationships

Service is doing for others—or allowing others to do for you—with no thought of reward on the part of the one serving. The joy of service is payment enough. To those who understand and appreciate giving, service is not an obligation—it's a privilege.

Service relationships are seen when people volunteer (or donate to) charities, visit people at hospices or hospitals, buy a meal (or a raincoat) for a homeless person, or so many other "senseless acts of kindness."

Ironically, the most selfish of relationships is, perhaps, serving others. It feels *so good* to do for others that it's difficult not to thank God they were in need, thus allowing us the pleasure of filling it.

There's not much to say about service relationships—if people know the joy of serving, they will include service in all their relationships.

Service relationships also allow others to serve us when we are in need. The old saying, "Don't return a favor, pass it on," was written to describe the receiving-end of service relationships.

Giving and receiving—it makes for powerful flow.

WALLPAPER DESIGN FOR
THE MARITAL BEDROOM

EXCUSE ME COULD YOU PLEASE SAY THAT AGAIN I DON'T BELIEVE I HEARD YOU CORRECTLY LISTEN JUST WHO THE HELL DO YOU THINK YOU ARE FOR GOD'S SAKE WHAT AM I SUPPOSED TO BE YOUR SERVANT DON'T YOU DARE TALK TO ME IN THAT TONE OF VOICE I GUESS WE JUST AREN'T MEANT TO BE TOGETHER THAT'S ALL I'VE HAD IT UP TO HERE WITH YOU THAT'S RIGHT YOU HEARD ME THAT'S NOT MEANT TO BE A THREAT WE'RE JUST IN DIFFERENT TIMES IN OUR LIFE OK GO AHEAD THEN LEAVE I'LL HELP YOU PACK YOUR BAGS I GUESS WE DON'T NEED TO BE TO-GETHER OH THAT'S CUTE REAL CUTE I DON'T HAVE TO STAND FOR

DAN GREENBURG
SUZANNE O'MALLEY

Marriage

Marriage, as a goal unto itself, is a difficult one—like making happiness a goal unto itself. Marriage, like all relationships, is a viable method for fulfilling certain goals. Most of the problems traditionally associated with marriage arise when people make marriage "the ideal goal" for *any* relationship that begins with physical attraction.

Most contracts are based on reasonable assumptions—or certainly include a great many of them—and most of the time these reasonable assumptions are reasonable enough. It's when one partner in the contract declares the other partner's demands unreasonable that trouble occurs.

As in marriage.

When people get married, the "marriage contract" is what the priest, rabbi, minister, or justice of the peace rattles off before each party proclaims "I do." Within that contract, however, is room for assumptions, misunderstandings, and unmet expectations galore.

Take the "love, honor, and cherish" part of many wedding ceremonies. *Sounds* very nice, but what does it *mean?* Oh! the marriages that have ended with a fight that began, "If you really loved me, you'd . . . ."

Far from the cultural myth that "being in love is enough" to make a marriage work, making a marriage work is a *lot* of work, and it begins by negotiating a proper contract. This begins with each party individually asking the question: "What do I want?"

> *I think a man can have two,*
> *maybe three affairs*
> *while he is married.*
>
> *But three is the absolute maximum.*
>
> *After that, you are cheating.*
>
> Yves Montand

If the answer to that question might include marriage as a *method* of getting what each wants, then the negotiations can continue. If not, bring on bachelor(ette) number two!

Some people want marriage in order to raise children—a perfectly reasonable (if not *the* most reasonable) reason for marriage. Others are looking for companionship, a tax break, financial support, insurance benefits, career advancements, or a host of other benefits. If children are high on one partner's list and completely absent from the other's, living in this marriage "made in heaven" could turn out to be hell-on-earth.

The problem of contradicting goals doesn't just apply to the desire to raise children, of course. If one partner, for example, sees extensive travel as part of the marriage, while the other wants to settle down on the organic farm they've always dreamed about, there will be unhappy tourists, unwatered turnips, and a marriage in which wanderlust and lust for the land will be in continual conflict.

Children—and organic farms—are twenty-four-hour-a-day-seven-day-a-week commitments. If a child, farm, travel, career, or an equally all-consuming desire dominates your wish list, make sure the subject is discussed and mutually understood *before* permanently partnering.

Both parties don't have to necessarily have the same goals. One party may say, "I have a major career goal, but if you want to have children, that's fine." To which the other party responds, "I understand that the children will be my responsibility. I appreciate your understanding and flexibility."

Marriage can be structured to fulfill almost any of the other types of relationships.

People can become such good friends and companions that marriage—with all its legal, social, and financial perks—might become the logical extension of a deepening love.

A power-point relationship could take the form of a marriage. Some people mistakenly call it a "traditional marriage" when they really mean a power-point relationship. Here the woman supports the man in his business goals (the man being the power-point), and the man supports the woman financially (and, in a more limited way, emotionally) in exchange for her support of his goals.

This is a perfectly workable power-point relation-

> *Passion,*
> *sexual passion,*
> *may lead to marriage,*
> *but cannot sustain marriage.*
>
> *The purpose of marriage*
> *is the raising of children,*
> *for which patience, not passion,*
> *is the necessary foundation.*
>
> EDWARD ABBEY

ship. When the "traditional marriage" people get involved, however, they make the mistake of assuming that the relationship must be heterosexual and male-centered, which eliminates the many successful relationships with the woman as the power-point and those with powerful same-sex partners. In the second place, they forget that not everyone wants a power-point relationship in the first place.

To say that power-point relationships can *only* be male-centered and heterosexual is absurd. Such claims become almost sacrilegious when these limited minds claim, "this is the only way God wants it."

Common-goal relationships make for good marriages—and seem to be especially suited for common goals such as raising children or opening Ma and Pa businesses. People sometimes say, with the requisite sadness in their voice, "They're only staying together for the children." Sometimes staying together for the children is far more satisfying than staying together simply because two people wanted to be together some time in the past—especially if the reason they wanted to be together was a physical attraction they don't much have anymore.

Ironically, the *least* reliable grounds for marriage is romance. Yes, the play you're watching may be very nice, but that's no reason to buy up the production and take all the actors home to live with you. If all that the actors do is perform the same play night after night, eventually it will get boring. (For you and the actors.)

The forty-six percent of marriages that *do* last longer than five years have almost all moved from being primarily romantic endeavors, to incorporating one or more of the other types of relationships.

But don't take my word for it—listen to . . .

Venus, a beautiful, good-natured lady, was the goddess of love; Juno, a terrible shrew, the goddess of marriage: and they were always mortal enemies.
    —*Jonathan Swift*

Are women books? says Hodge, then would mine were an Almanack, to change her every year.
    —*Benjamin Franklin*

One good Husband is worth two good wives, for the scarcer things are the more they're valued.
    —*Benjamin Franklin*

> *It's an extra dividend*
> *when you like the girl*
> *you're in love with.*
>
> CLARK GABLE

A good marriage, if there is such a thing, rejects the company and conditions of love. It tries to imitate those of friendship.—*Michel de Montaigne*

I would like to be like my father and all the rest of my ancestors who never married.—*Molière*

Marriage, in life, is like a duel in the midst of a battle.
—*Edmond About*

In matters of religion and matrimony I never give advice; because I will have no man's torments in this world or the next laid to my charge.
—*Lord Chesterfield*

There are some good marriages, but practically no delightful ones.—*La Rochefoucauld*

One exists with one's husband—one lives with one's lover.—*Balzac*

Love is a reciprocity of soul and has a different end and obeys different laws from marriage. Hence one should not take the loved one to wife.
   —*Alessandro Piccolomini*

Passion and marriage are essentially irreconcilable. Their origins and their ends make them mutually exclusive. Their co-existence in our midst constantly raises insoluble problems, and the strife thereby engendered constitutes a persistent danger for every one of our social safeguards.
   —*Denis de Rougemont*

Spouses are impediments to great enterprises.
   —*Sir Francis Bacon*

Marriage must incessantly contend with a monster that devours everything: familiarity.—*Balzac*

A system could not well have been devised more studiously hostile to human happiness than marriage.
   —*Percy Bysshe Shelley*

'Tis the established custom (in Vienna) for every lady to have two husbands, one that bears the name and another that performs the duties.
   —*Mary Wortley Montagu*

It is most unwise for people in love to marry.
   —*George Bernard Shaw*

I feel sure that no girl could go to the altar, and would probably *refuse*, if she knew all . . . .
   —*Queen Victoria*

I would not marry God.—*Maxine Elliott (telegram denying rumors of her marriage)*

> *I never loved another person
> the way I loved myself.*
>
> MAE WEST

It destroys one's nerves to be amiable every day to the same human being.—*Benjamin Disraeli*

What God hath joined together no man shall put asunder: God will take care of that.
   —*George Bernard Shaw*

At the beginning of a marriage ask yourself whether this woman will be interesting to talk to from now until old age. Everything else in marriage is transitory: most of the time is spent in conversation.—*Friedrich Nietzsche*

I have certainly seen more men destroyed by the desire to have a wife and child and to keep them in comfort than I have seen destroyed by drink or harlots.—*William Butler Yeats*

Any intelligent woman who reads the marriage contract, and then goes into it, deserves all the consequences.—*Isadora Duncan*

Love is an obsessive delusion that is cured by marriage.—*Dr. Karl Bowman*

A word which should be pronounced "mirage."
—*Herbert Spencer*

If married couples did not live together, happy marriages would be more frequent.—*Nietzsche*

In our part of the world where monogamy is the rule, to marry means to halve one's rights and double one's duties.—*Schopenhauer*

He had been building one of those piles of thought, as ramshackle and fantastic as a Chinese pagoda, half from words let fall by gentlemen in gaiters, half from the litter in his own mind, about duck shooting and legal history, about the Roman occupation of Lincoln and the relations of country gentlemen with their wives, when, from all this disconnected rambling, there suddenly formed itself in his mind the idea that he would ask Mary to marry him.—*Virginia Woolf*

Nothing anybody tells you about marriage helps.—*Max Siegel*

Not all women give most of their waking thoughts to the problem of pleasing men. Some are married.—*Emma Lee*

I've sometimes thought of marrying, and then I've thought again.—*Noel Coward*

I cannot see myself as a wife—ugly word.
—*Greta Garbo*

> *She cried—*
> *and the judge wiped her tears*
> *with my checkbook.*

TOMMY MANVILLE
THIRTEEN-TIMES-DIVORCED MILLIONAIRE

I was in rare fettle and the heart had touched a new high. I don't know anything that braces one up like finding you haven't got to get married after all.—*P. G. Wodehouse*

The difficulty with marriage is that we fall in love with a personality, but must live with a character.—*Peter DeVries*

AREN'T YOU FORGETTING YOU'RE MARRIED?
Mae West: Hmmm—I'm doing my best.

American women expect to find in their husbands a perfection that English women only hope to find in their butlers.—*W. Somerset Maugham*

I was married by a judge. I should have asked for a jury.—*George Burns*

Before marriage, a man declares that he would lay down his life to serve you; after marriage, he won't even lay down his newspaper to talk to you.

—*Helen Rowland*

I should never have married, but I didn't want to live without a man. Brought up to respect the conventions, love had to end in marriage. I'm afraid it did.—*Bette Davis*

Marriage is a bribe to make a housekeeper think she's a householder.—*Thornton Wilder*

Take it from me, marriage isn't a word—it's a sentence.—*King Vidor*

Only choose in marriage a woman whom you would choose as a friend if she were a man.

—*Joseph Joubert*

People marry for a variety of reasons, and with varying results; but to marry for love is to invite inevitable tragedy.—*James Branch Cabell*

Politics doesn't make strange bedfellows—marriage does.—*Groucho Marx*

Do you know what it means to come home at night to a woman who'll give you a little love, a little affection, a little tenderness? It means you're in the wrong house, that's what it means.

—*Henny Youngman*

We do not squabble, fight or have rows. We collect grudges. We're in an arms race, storing up warheads for the domestic Armageddon.

—*Hugh Leonard*

If you want to read about love and marriage you've got to buy two separate books.—*Alan King*

> *I don't think there are any men
> who are faithful to their wives.*
>
> JACQUELINE KENNEDY ONASSIS

> *Husbands are chiefly good lovers
> when they are betraying their wives.*
>
> MARILYN MONROE

My wife was in labor with our first child for thirty-two hours and I was faithful to her the whole time.—*Jonathan Katz*

ERIC: She's a lovely girl . . .
I'd like to marry her,
but her family objects.
ERNIE: Her family?
ERIC: Yes, her husband and four kids.
 —*Eric Morecambe and Ernie Wise*

Alcestis had exercised a mysterious attraction and then an unmysterious repulsion on two former husbands, the second of whom had to resort to fatal coronary disease to get away from her.
 —*Kingsley Amis*

I'd like to get married because I like the idea of a man being required by law to sleep with me every night.—*Carrie Snow*

Marriage is really tough because you have to deal with feelings and lawyers.—*Richard Pryor*

Being a bachelor is the first requisite of the man who wishes to form an ideal home.
    —*Beverly Nichols*

I belong to Bridegrooms Anonymous. Whenever I feel like getting married, they send over a lady in a housecoat and hair curlers to burn my toast for me.—*Dick Martin*

When a girl marries she exchanges the attentions of many men for the inattention of one.
    —*Helen Rowland*

A man in love is incomplete until he is married. Then he is finished.—*Zsa Zsa Gabor*

The act of getting married, stripped of the necessity to have a secure setting to raise children, seems to me no less grim than registering your emotions with the government.—*Harry Shearer*

I want a man who's kind and understanding. Is that too much to ask of a millionaire?
    —*Zsa Zsa Gabor*

Even under the best of circumstances men are hard creatures to trap. Women who flatter themselves into thinking they've trapped one are like people who believe they can get rid of the cockroaches in their kitchen. They're in for a big surprise late one night when they turn on the light.
    —*Harry Shearer*

> *When a couple decide to divorce,*
> *they should inform both sets of parents*
> *before having a party*
> *and telling all their friends.*
>
> *This is not only courteous but practical.*
>
> *Parents may be very willing*
> *to pitch in with comments, criticism*
> *and malicious gossip of their own*
> *to help the divorce along.*
>
> P. J. O'ROURKE

I don't think I'll get married again. I'll just find a woman I don't like and give her a house.
—*Lewis Grizzard*

I am a marvelous housekeeper. Every time I leave a man I keep his house.—*Zsa Zsa Gabor*

I love being married. It's so great to find that one special person you want to annoy for the rest of your life.—*Rita Rudner*

Marriage is a great institution, but I'm not ready for an institution yet.—*Mae West*

I'd marry again if I found a man who had $15 million and would sign over half of it to me before the marriage, and guarantee that he'd be dead within a year.—*Bette Davis*

Far from being the basis of the good society, the family, with its narrow privacy and tawdry secrets, is the source of all our discontents.
—*Sir Edmund Leach*

The Family! Home of all social evils, a charitable institution for indolent women, a prison workshop for the slaving breadwinner, and a hell for children.
—*August Strindberg (1886)*

We sleep in separate rooms, we have dinner apart, we take separate vacations—we're doing everything we can to keep our marriage together.
—*Rodney Dangerfield*

The happiest time in any man's life is just after the first divorce.—*John Kenneth Galbraith*

*You grow up
the day you have
your first
real laugh
—at yourself.*

Ethel Barrymore

Laughter—
The Shortcut to Self-Love

How do I end a book on self-loving? I do not have an answer to that question. I only have one more bit of advice to offer (laugh a lot), and a pile of perfectly wonderful quotes that failed to find a home in previous chapters.

All I can do, then, is give you the best of these self-loving quotes while praising the joys of humor, and pray this will make a smooth transition from my loving you (I hope you felt it) to you loving you. I'd better move on to the humor before my love-poet personality surfaces again and begins writing you an ode. Take good care.

> At twilight nature becomes a wonderfully suggestive effect, and is not without loveliness, though perhaps its chief use is to illustrate quotations from the poets.—*Oscar Wilde*

> Laughter is man's most distinctive emotional expression. Man shares the capacity for love and hate, anger and fear, loyalty and grief, with other living creatures. But humor, which has an intellectual as well as an emotional element, belongs to man.—*Margaret Mead*

> When a woman unhappily yoked talks about the soul with a man not her husband, it isn't the soul they are talking about.—*Don Marquis*

> Never be possessive. If a female friend lets on that she is going out with another man, be kind and understanding. If she says she would like to go out

> *Not a shred of evidence*
> *exists in favor*
> *of the idea*
> *that life is serious.*
>
> BRENDAN GILL

with the Dallas Cowboys, including the coaching staff, the same rule applies. Tell her: "Kath, you just go right ahead and do what you feel is right." Unless you actually care for her, in which case you must see to it that she has no male contact whatsoever.—*Bruce Jay Friedman*

I said to the wife, "Guess what I heard in the pub? They reckon the milkman has made love to every woman in this road except one." And she said, "I'll bet it's that stuck-up Phyllis at number 23."
　—*Max Kauffmann*

Life's more amusing than we thought.
　—*Andrew Long*

Never get a mime talking. He won't stop.
　—*Marcel Marceau*

I hate to be a failure. I hate and regret the failure of my marriages. I would gladly give all my millions for just one lasting marital success.

    —*J. Paul Getty*

Those who have some means think that the most important thing in the world is love. The poor know that it is money.—*Gerald Brenan*

You *dare* to dicker with your pontiff?

    —*Rex Harrison to Charlton Heston,*
      The Agony and the Ecstasy

Isn't there any other part of the matzo you can eat?—*Marilyn Monroe (when served matzo ball soup three times in a row)*

It is ridiculous to think you can spend your entire life with just one person. Three is about the right number. Yes, I imagine three husbands would do it.—*Clare Boothe Luce*

I think every woman is entitled to a middle husband she can forget.—*Adela Rogers St. John*

On stage I make love to 25,000 people; then I go home alone.—*Janis Joplin*

I'm saving the bass player for Omaha.—*Janis Joplin*

In bed my real love has always been the sleep that rescued me by allowing me to dream.

    —*Luigi Pirandello*

Believe nothing, no matter where you read it, or who said it—even if I have said it—unless it agrees with your own reason and your own common sense.—*The Buddha*

Beware of the man who denounces women writers; his penis is tiny & cannot spell.—*Erica Jong*

> *Imagination*
> *is a quality given a man*
> *to compensate him*
> *for what he is not,*
> *and a sense of humor*
> *was provided*
> *to console him*
> *for what he is.*
>
> OSCAR WILDE

His mother should have thrown him away and kept the stork.—*Mae West*

Don't take yourself too seriously. And don't be too serious about not taking yourself too seriously.
   —*Howard Ogden*

A difference of taste in jokes is a great strain on the affections.—*George Eliot*

EVER MEET A MAN THAT COULD MAKE YOU HAPPY?
Mae West: Several times.

When a Roman was returning from a trip, he used to send someone ahead to let his wife know, so as not to surprise her in the act.—*Montaigne*

Seriousness is the only refuge of the shallow.
   —*Oscar Wilde*

The psychology of adultery has been falsified by conventional morals, which assume, in monogamous countries, that attraction to one person cannot coexist with affection for another. Everybody knows that this is untrue.—*Bertrand Russell*

Your idea of fidelity is not having more than one man in bed at the same time.—*Frederic Raphael*

GEORGE S. KAUFMAN: I like your bald head, Marc. It feels just like my wife's behind.

MARC CONNOLLY (feeling his head): So it does, George, so it does.

Humor must be one of the chief attributes of God. Plants and animals that are distinctly humorous in form and characteristics are God's jokes.
   —*Mark Twain*

We can call each other girls, chicks, broads, birds and dames with equanimity. Many of us prefer to do so since the word "woman," being two syllables, is long, unwieldy, and earnest. But a man must watch his ass. Never may a man be permitted to call any female a "chick." He may call you a broad or a dame only if he is a close friend and fond of John Garfield movies. The term "bird," generally used by fatuous Englishmen, is always frowned upon.—*Cynthia Heimel*

LADY ASTOR: If you were my husband, Winston, I'd put poison in your tea.

WINSTON CHURCHILL: If I were your husband, Nancy, I'd drink it.

I love tranquil solitude
And such society
As is quite, wise, and good.
   —*Percy Bysshe Shelley*

> *The one important thing*
> *I have learned over the years*
> *is the difference between*
> *taking one's work seriously*
> *and taking one's self seriously.*
>
> *The first is imperitive and*
> *the second is disastrous.*

MARGOT FONTEYN

A good and wholesome thing is a little harmless fun in this world; it tones a body up and keeps him human and prevents him from souring.
— *Mark Twain*

It doesn't matter who gives them as long as you never wear anything second-rate. Wait for the first-class jewels, Gigi. Hold on to your ideals.—*Collette*

A full bosom is actually a millstone around a woman's neck; it endears her to the men who want to make their mammet of her, but she is never allowed to think that their popping eyes actually see her.—*Germaine Greer*

The hardest years in life are those between ten and seventy.—*Helen Hayes (at age eighty-three)*

I've made so many movies playing a hooker that they don't pay me in the regular way any more. They leave it on the dresser.—*Shirley MacLaine*

One popular new plastic surgery technique is called lipgrafting, or "fat recycling," wherein fat cells are removed from one part of your body that is too large, such as your buttocks, and injected into your lips; people will then be literally kissing your ass.—*Dave Barry*

WIFE: Mr. Watt next door blows his wife a kiss
every morning as he leaves the house.
I wish you'd do that.
HUSBAND: But I hardly know the woman!
—*Alfred McFote*

Love is the self-delusion we manufacture to justify the trouble we take to have sex.—*Dan Greenburg*

A LEXICON FOR FIGHTING MARITAL FIGHTS,
ARRANGED ACCORDING TO SUBJECT

Amnesia: "Who do you think you ARE?"

Apology: "PARdon me for LIVing!"

Family Tree: "She's YOUR mother, not mine."

Hearing impairments: "Could you speak up a little? They can't hear you in Europe."

Language barrier: "What's the matter, don't you understand English?"

Mining: "I hadn't realized we'd descended to that level."

Wildlife: "That's right, use physical violence. That's all an animal like you knows anyway."

—*Dan Greenburg and Suzanne O'Malley*

> *Laughter*
> *is an orgasm*
> *triggered by the intercourse*
> *of reason with unreason.*
>
> JACK KROLL

I have a big flaw in that I am attracted to thin, tall, good-looking men who have one common denominator. They must be lurking bastards.
—*Edna O'Brien*

He speaks to me as if I were a public meeting.
—*Queen Victoria (about Gladstone)*

Mirth is the sweet wine of human life. It should be offered sparkling with zestful life unto God.
—*Henry Ward Beecher*

For some of the large indignities of life, the best remedy is direct action. For the small indignities, the best remedy is a Charlie Chaplin movie.
—*Carol Tavris*

Laughter is the tonic, the relief, the surcease for pain.—*Charlie Chaplin*

It's relaxing to go out with my ex-wife because she already knows I'm an idiot.—*Warren Thomas*

The nurse of full-grown souls is solitude.
—*James Russell Lowell (1844)*

To say that you can love one person all your life is just like saying that one candle will continue burning as long as you live.—*Leo Tolstoy*

The chief cause of unhappiness in married life is that people think that marriage is sex attraction, which takes the form of promises and hopes and happiness—a view supported by public opinion and by literature. But marriage cannot cause happiness. Instead, it is always torture, which man has to pay for satisfying his sex urge.—*Leo Tolstoy*

Why do you always, when you mention my name in your diaries, speak so ill of me? Why do you want all future generations and our descendants to hold my name in contempt? Are you afraid that your glory after death will be diminished unless you show me to have been your torment and yourself as a martyr, bearing a cross in the form of your wife?—*Sonya Tolstoy (in a letter to her husband)*

In 1910, eighty-two-year-old Leo Tolstoy flees from his wife and dies in a railway station of exposure.—*Jon Winokur*

Men and women, women and men. It will never work.—*Erica Jong*

Older woman younger man! Popular wisdom claims that this particular class of love affair is the most poignant, tender, poetic, exquisite one there is, altogether the choicest on the menu.
—*Doris Lessing*

> *The only difference*
> *between a caprice*
> *and a lifelong passion*
> *is that a caprice*
> *lasts a little longer.*
>
> OSCAR WILDE

WHAT TO DO WITH YOUR TIME AFTER BEING DUMPED

DO: *Drink black coffee and smoke numerous cigs. You NEED to eat and this will do. *Find out who "she" is and introduce yourself. Scrutinize her appearance and comfort yourself with thoughts of her large pores or taste in clothes. *Drink mass quantities of alcohol and watch TV all you can. *Abandon personal hygiene and cleaning your house. *Kick his car.

DON'T: *Take up a new hobby. When the most hellish period has passed you will be unable to do this activity ever again in your life. *Try to meet a new lovemate through church organizations or night

classes in ballroom dancing. *Try to feel
happy or good for thirty days. *Go anywhere or do anything. *Go near high
bridges, open windows, trucks that are
moving fast or couples holding hands.
—*Lynda Barry*

I have had my belly full of great men (forgive the
expression). I quite like to read about them in the
pages of Plutarch, where they don't outrage my
humanity. Let us see them carved in marble or cast
in bronze, and hear no more about them. In real
life they are nasty creatures, persecutors, tempera-
mental, despotic, bitter and suspicious.
—*George Sand*

To err is human—but it feels divine.—*Mae West*

Most conversations are simply monologues deliv-
ered in the presence of a witness.—*Margaret Millar*

The opposite of talking isn't listening. The opposite of talking is waiting.—*Fran Lebowitz*

I hope that one or two immortal lyrics will come
out of all this tumbling around.—*Poet Louise Bogan
on her love affair with poet Theodore Roethke*

The perfect lover is one who turns into a pizza at
4:00 A.M.—*Charles Pierce*

You do not need to leave your room. Remain sitting at your table and listen. Do not even listen,
simply wait. Do not even wait, be quite still and
solitary. The world will freely offer itself to you to
be unmasked, it has no choice, it will roll in ecstasy at your feet.—*Franz Kafka*

It's lavish, but I call it home.
—*Clifton Webb to Dana Andrews, <u>Laura</u> (1944)*

> *My problem*
> *is intense vanity*
> *and narcissism.*
>
> *I've always had*
> *such a good physique*
> *and such intense charm*
> *that it's difficult*
> *to be true to myself.*
>
> LAWRENCE DURRELL

A narcissist is someone better looking than you are.—*Gore Vidal*

What is a promiscuous person? It's usually someone who is getting more sex than you are.
   —*Victor Lownes*

Voyeurism is a healthy, non-participatory sexual activity—the world *should* look at the world.
   —*Desmond Morris*

Sex is like having dinner: sometimes you joke about the dishes, sometimes you take the meal seriously.—*Woody Allen*

Since Time is not a person we can overtake when he is gone, let us honor him with mirth and cheerfulness of heart while he is passing.—*Goethe*

The first and simplest emotion which we discover in the human mind, is curiosity.—*Edmund Burke*

Abstainer, *n.* A weak person who yields to the temptation of denying himself a pleasure.
   —*Ambrose Bierce*

She gave me a smile I could feel in my hip pocket.—*Raymond Chandler*

I can understand companionship. I can understand bought sex in the afternoon. I cannot understand the love affair.— *Gore Vidal*

Humor is laughing at what you haven't got when you ought to have it.—*Langston Hughes*

Love is the same as *like* except you feel sexier. And more romantic. And also more annoyed when he talks with his mouth full. And you also resent it more when he interrupts you. And you also respect him less when he shows any weakness. And furthermore, when you ask him to pick you up at the airport and he tells you he can't do it because he's busy, it's only when you love him that you hate him.—*Judith Viorst*

Out upon it, I have loved
Three whole days together;
And am like to love three more,
If it prove fair weather.
   —*Sir John Suckling (1646)*

When you're in love it's the most glorious two-and-a-half days of your life.—*Richard Lewis*

Love without attachment is light.
   —*Norman O. Brown*

If you want to make a friend, let someone do you a favor.—*Benjamin Franklin*

> *I'm no angel,*
> *but I've*
> *spread my wings a bit.*
>
> MAE WEST

The artist who aims at perfection in everything achieves it in nothing.—*Delacroix*

I don't continually question my reason to live. It's just a state of being. The real question is what you're doing with the living you're doing, and what you want to do with that living.—*Mick Jagger*

Humor, in all its many-splendored varieties, can be simply defined as a type of stimulation which tends to elicit the laughter reflex.—*Arthur Koestler*

I wrote the story myself. It's all about a girl who lost her reputation but never missed it.—*Mae West*

The lovely thing about being forty is that you can appreciate twenty-five-year-old men more.
    —*Colleen McCullough*

To be free is to have achieved your life.
    —*Tennessee Williams*

Free your mind and your ass will follow.
    —*George Clinton*

A man is too apt to forget that in this world he cannot have everything. A choice is all that is left him.—*H. Mathews*

It is explained that all relationships require a—little give and take. This is untrue. Any partnership demands that we give and give and give and at the last, as we flop into our graves exhausted, we are told that we didn't give enough.—*Quentin Crisp*

Only the really plain people know about love. The very fascinating ones try so hard to create an impression that they soon exhaust their talents.
    —*Katharine Hepburn*

Only the untalented can afford to be humble.
    —*Sylvia Miles*

I am a disciplined comedian; of course I take direction. From God, that is.—*Spike Milligan*

Some say life is the thing, but I prefer reading.
    —*Ruth Rendell*

Custom is the plague of wise men and the idol of fools.—*Thomas Fuller*

Familiar acts are beautiful through love.
    —*Percy Bysshe Shelley*

Children today are tyrants. They contradict their parents, gobble their food, and tyrannize their teachers.—*Socrates*

Egotist, *n.* A person of low taste, more interested in himself than in me.—*Ambrose Bierce*

> *Humor is vague,*
> *runaway stuff*
> *that hisses*
> *around the fissures*
> *and crevices*
> *of the mind,*
> *like some sort*
> *of loose physic gas.*
>
> JONATHAN MILLER

Always obey your superiors—if you have any.
—*Mark Twain*

Dare to be naive.—*R. Buckminster Fuller*

I recommend having no relationships except those easily borne and disposed of; I recommend limiting one's involvement in other people's lives to a pleasantly scant minimum.—*Quentin Crisp*

Do not fear when your enemies criticize you. Beware when they applaud.—*Vo Dong Giang*

If an idea is important enough it is worth laughing at.—*Alan Plater*

An effort impelled by desire must also have an automatic or subconscious energy to aid its realization.—*Man Ray*

Thousands have lived without love, not one without water.—*W. H. Auden*

Once you know what women are like, men get kind of boring. I'm not trying to put them down, I mean I like them sometimes as people, but sexually they're dull.—*Rita Mae Brown*

Most of our platitudes notwithstanding, self-deception remains the most difficult deception. The tricks that work on others count for nothing in that very well-lit back alley where one keeps assignations with oneself: no winning smiles will do here, no prettily drawn lists of good intentions.
   —*Joan Didion*

The greatest thing in the world is to know how to belong to oneself.
   —*Michel Eyquem de Montaigne (1580)*

No one is born prejudiced against others, but everyone is born prejudiced in favor of himself.
   —*David Stafford-Clark, M.D.*

In April, if the glands work properly, it is possible to see the world as it might be if only it were not the world.—*Russell Baker*

That inward eye
Which is the bliss of solitude.
   —*William Wordsworth (1807)*

When the mind's eye turns inward, it blazes upon the dearly beloved image of oneself.—*Fannie Hurst*

Experience shows that success is due less to ability than to zeal. The winner is he who gives himself to his work, body and soul.—*Charles Buxton*

"Do-so" is more important than "say-so."
   —*Pete Seeger*

> *We are made out of oppositions;*
> *we live between two poles—*
> *you don't reconcile the poles,*
> *you just recognize them.*

> ORSON WELLES

Men would like to love themselves but they usually find that they cannot. That is because they have built an ideal image of themselves which puts their real self in the shade.—*Gerald Brenan*

The first and worst of all frauds is to cheat oneself.—*Gamaliel Bailey*

The world is divided into two classes, those who believe the incredible, and those who do the improbable.—*Oscar Wilde*

Nature is an infinite sphere whose center is everywhere and whose circumference is nowhere.
—*Blaise Pascal*

It's the good girls who keep the diaries; the bad girls never have the time.—*Tallulah Bankhead*

Never underestimate a man who overestimates himself.—*Franklin D. Roosevelt*

Art is a jealous mistress, and if a man has a genius for painting, poetry, music, architecture or philosophy, he makes a bad husband and an ill provider.
—*Ralph Waldo Emerson*

Satisfaction will come to those who please themselves.—*Arnold Lobel*

All men are frauds. The only difference between them is that some admit it. I myself deny it.
—*H. L. Mencken*

Any life, no matter how long and complex it may be, is made up of a *single moment*—the moment in which a man finds out, once and for all, who he is.—*Jorge Luis Borges*

In seeking truth you have to get both sides of a story.—*Walter Cronkite*

The chief ingredients in the composition of those qualities that gain esteem and praise, are good nature, truth, good sense, and good breeding.
—*Joseph Addison*

Make the most of yourself, for that is all there is of you.—*Ralph Waldo Emerson*

Characters do not change. Opinions alter, but characters are only developed.—*Benjamin Disraeli*

Evolution is the law of life, and there is no evolution save toward Individualism.—*Oscar Wilde*

People become who they are. Even Beethoven became Beethoven.—*Randy Newman*

We are the products of editing, rather than authorship.—*George Wald*

> MOTHER: *Do you love me, Albert?*
>
> ALBERT: *Yes.*
>
> MOTHER: *Yes—what?*
>
> ALBERT: *Yes, please.*
>
> TOM STOPPARD

It is better to be hated for what you are than loved for what you are not.—*Andre Gide*

With people of only moderate ability modesty is mere honesty; but with those who possess great talent it is hypocrisy.—*Arthur Schopenhauer*

The legs aren't so beautiful, I just know what to do with them.—*Marlene Dietrich*

All my shows are great. Some of them are bad. But they're all great.—*Lord Grade*

The world will never starve for want of wonders, but for want of wonder.—*G. K. Chesterton*

God enters by a private door into every individual.—*Ralph Waldo Emerson*

The best way to know God is to love many things.—*Vincent van Gogh*

What good is it for a man to gain the whole world, and yet lose or forfeit his very self?
—*Jesus of Nazareth (Luke 9:25)*

There is surely a piece of divinity in us, something that was before the elements, and owes no homage unto the sun.—*Sir Thomas Browne (1642)*

There are only two ways to live your life. One is as though nothing is a miracle. The other is as though everything is a miracle.—*Albert Einstein*

Dignity consists not in possessing honors, but in the consciousness that we deserve them.—*Aristotle*

What the world needs is more geniuses with humility. There are so few of us left.—*Oscar Levant*

Would you hurt a man keenest, strike at his self-love.—*Lew Wallace, Ben Hur (1880)*

There's a story about President and Mrs. Coolidge visiting a poultry show. The guide says to Mrs. Coolidge, "You know, ma'am, the rooster here performs his services up to eight or nine times a day," to which the First Lady replied, "Please see to it that the President is given that information!" A while later the President's party came through the same exhibit and the guide told him, "Sir, Mrs. Coolidge said to be sure to tell you that the rooster there performs his services up to eight or nine times a day." Coolidge thought for a moment and asked, "Same chicken each time?" "No, Mr. President, different chickens each time." "Then see to it that Mrs. Coolidge is given *that* information!"
—*Orson Bean*

> *I believe that order is better than chaos, creation better than destruction. I prefer gentleness to violence, forgiveness to vendetta . . . I think knowledge is preferable to ignorance and I am sure that human sympathy is more valuable than ideology . . . And I think we should remember we are part of a great whole, which for convenience we call nature. All living things are our brothers and sisters. Above all I believe in the God-given genius of certain individuals, and I value a society that makes their existence possible.*

SIR KENNETH CLARK

Self-confidence is the first requisite to great undertakings.—*Dr. Samuel Johnson*

I have great faith in fools—self-confidence my friends call it.—*Edgar Allan Poe*

He always did have that "Touch of Madness" that marks the true artist and breaks the hearts of the young girls from fine homes.—*Robert Crumb*

Delight is to him—a far, far upward, and inward delight—who against the proud gods and commodores of this earth, ever stands forth his own inexorable self.—*Herman Melville, Moby Dick (1851)*

Man who man would be,
Must rule the empire of himself.
    —*Percy Bysshe Shelley*

Anybody can become angry—that is easy; but to be angry with the right person, and to the right degree, and at the right time, and for the right purpose, and in the right way—that is not within everybody's power and is not easy.—*Aristotle*

An occasional compliment is necessary, to keep up one's self-respect. When you cannot get a compliment any other way, pay yourself one.
   —*Mark Twain*

A few strong instincts and a few plain rules suffice us.—*Ralph Waldo Emerson*

We must learn to distinguish morality from moralizing.—*Henry Kissinger*

Understanding a person does not mean condoning; it only means that one does not accuse him as if one were God or a judge placed above him.
   —*Erich Fromm*

Let people push you around. The person who says, believes, and acts on the phrase "I ain't taking any shit from anybody" is a very busy person indeed. This person must be ever vigilant against news vendors who shortchange him, cab drivers who take him the wrong way around, waiters who serve the other guy first, florists who are charging ten cents more per tulip than the one down the block, pharmacists who make you wait too long and cars that cut you off at the light: they are a veritable miasma of righteous indignation and never have a minute to relax and have a good time.—*Cynthia Heimel*

You never will be the person you can be if pressure, tension, and discipline are taken out of your life.—*James G. Bilkey*

> *Dear Miss Manners,*
>
> *What am I supposed to say when I am introduced to a homosexual couple?*
>
> *Gentle Reader,*
>
> *"How do you do?"*
> *"How do you do?"*
>
> JUDITH MARTIN

I know the answer! The answer lies within the heart of all mankind! The answer is twelve? I think I'm in the wrong building.
—*Lucy van Pelt, "Peanuts"*

Any preoccupation with ideas of what is right or wrong in conduct shows an arrested intellectual development.—*Oscar Wilde*

The genitals themselves have not undergone the development of the rest of the human form in the direction of beauty.—*Sigmund Freud*

In 453, Attila the Hun died from a nosebleed on his wedding night.—*Jon Winokur*

Zeal is very blind, or badly regulated, when it encroaches upon the rights of others.—*Quesnel*

There is no dependence that can be sure but a dependence upon one's self.—*John Gay*

When the freedom they wished for most was freedom from responsibility, then Athens ceased to be free and was never free again.—*Edith Hamilton*

Self-abuse is the most certain road to the grave.
   —*George M. Calhoun, M.D. (1855)*

Hey, don't knock masturbation. It's sex with someone I love.—*Woody Allen*

Masturbation! The amazing availability of it!
   —*James Joyce*

Why don't you write books people can read?
   —*Nora Joyce (to her husband, James)*

A woman occasionally is quite a serviceable substitute for masturbation. It takes an abundance of imagination, to be sure.—*Karl Kraus*

I like making love myself and I can make love for about *three minutes*. Three minutes and I need eight hours sleep, and a bowl of Wheaties.
   —*Richard Pryor*

DORIS DAY (to Rock Hudson): Mr. Allen, this may come as a shock to you, but there are some men who don't end every sentence with a proposition.—*Pillow Talk*

For flavor, instant sex will never supersede the stuff you have to peel and cook.—*Quentin Crisp*

Let's take coitus out of the closet and off the altar and put it in the continuum of human behaviour.—*John Updike*

Believe those who are seeking the truth; doubt those who find it.—*Andre Gide*

> *Whoever undertakes*
> *to set himself up*
> *as a judge*
> *in the field of truth*
> *and knowledge*
> *is shipwrecked*
> *by the laughter of the Gods.*
>
> ALBERT EINSTEIN

Truth has no special time of its own. Its hour is now—always.—*Albert Schweitzer*

We cannot be *normal* and *alive* at the same time.
—*E. M. Cioran*

My sense of my own importance to myself is tremendous. I am all I have, to work with, to play with, to suffer and to enjoy. It is not the eyes of others that I am wary of, but my own.
—*Noel Coward*

He fell in love with himself at first sight and it is a passion to which he has always been faithful.
—*Anthony Powell*

Tolerance is the oil which takes the friction out of life.—*Wilbert E. Scheer*

Such tendency toward doing good as is in men's hearts would not be diminished by the removal of the delusion that good deeds are primarily for the sake of No. 2 instead of for the sake of No. 1.

—*Mark Twain*

Your responsibility as a parent is not as great as you might imagine. You need not supply the world with the next conqueror of disease or major motion picture star. If your child simply grows up to be someone who does not use the word "collectible" as a noun, you can consider yourself an unqualified success.—*Fran Lebowitz*

You can't be happy with a woman who pronounces both *d*'s in Wednesday.—*Peter De Vries*

Ecstasy cannot last, but it can carve a channel for something lasting.—*E.M. Forster.*

To dry one's eyes and laugh at a fall,
And baffled, get up and begin again.
   —*Robert Browning (1855)*

*Reading is like
permitting a man
to talk a long time,
and refusing you
the right to answer.*

ED HOWE

*When I am dead,
I hope it may be said:
"His sins were scarlet,
but his books were read."*

HILAIRE BELLOC

Other Books by Peter McWilliams

LOVE 101 Audio Tapes

The complete, unabridged book on audio tapes, read by the author. Includes old songs and lots of fun. $24.95.

DO IT! Let's Get Off Our Buts

This is a book for those who want to discover—clearly and precisely—their dream; how to pursue that dream, even if it means learning (and—gasp!—practicing) some new behavior; and who wouldn't mind having some fun along the way. 500 pages. **Paperback,** $5.95. **Audio tapes** (unabridged), six cassettes, $24.95.

LIFE 102: What to Do When Your Guru Sues You

This book is presented as a moral tale—the journey of a New Age Candide—that explores the dangers of uninvited programming. It even includes lessons on how to counter-program and reprogram destructive programming, be it from a cult leader, a relative, the Tobacco Institute, or yourself. Peter McWilliams explains what we can do to obtain and maintain our personal freedom—a risky but rewarding task. 424 pages. **Hardcover,** $19.95.

You Can't Afford the Luxury of a Negative Thought

This is a book for anyone afflicted with one of the primary diseases of our time: negative thinking. 622 pages. **Paperback,** $5.95. **Audio tapes** (unabridged, eight cassettes), $24.95. **Wristwatch,** $35.00.

Focus on the Positive

Exercises, processes, journal space, drawing room, and more—all designed to complement the material in the preceding book. 200 pages. **Trade paperback,** $11.95.

LIFE 101: Everything We Wish We Had Learned About Life In School—But Didn't

The overview book of The LIFE 101 SERIES. The idea behind LIFE 101 is that everything in life is for our upliftment, learning and growth—including (and, perhaps especially) the "bad" stuff. "The title jolly well says it all," said the Los Angeles Times—jolly well saying it all. 480 pages. **Trade paperback,** $5.95. **Audio tapes** (unabridged, five cassettes), $22.95. **Wristwatch,** $35.00

WEALTH 101: Wealth Is Much More Than Money

First, *WEALTH 101* explores, in detail, how to enjoy the life you already have. From that foundation of appreciation and gratitude, we explore how to obtain more of what you really want. 532 pages. **Trade paperback,** $11.95. **Audio tapes** (unabridged, eight cassettes), $22.95.

How to Heal Depression

by Harold H. Bloomfield, M.D., and Peter McWilliams

The first companion book of the eighteen-year bestseller, *How to Survive the Loss of a Love*. In simple, clear, direct prose (with quotes on every other page) it explains what depression is, what causes it, and what the most effective treatments are. **Hardcover,** $14.95. **Audio tapes** (unabridged, read by the authors), $15.95.

How to Survive the Loss of a Love

by Melba Colgrove, Ph.D., Harold H. Bloomfield, M.D.,
and Peter McWilliams

A directly helpful guide to recovery from any loss or major change in life. 212 pages. **Hardcover,** $10. **Trade paperback** (rack size), $5.95. **Audio tapes** (unabridged, two cassettes, read by the authors), $11.95.

Surviving, Healing and Growing
The How to Survive the Loss of a Love Workbook

Exercises, processes, and suggestions designed to supplement *How to Survive the Loss of a Love*. Lots of room to write, draw, doodle, survive, heal & grow. 200 pages. **Trade paperback,** $11.95.

Come Love With Me & Be My Life
The Complete Romantic Poetry of Peter McWilliams

Touching, direct, emotional, often funny, this is the best of Peter McWilliams's romantic poetry. 250 pages. **Hardcover,** $12.95. **Audio tapes** (unabridged, two cassettes, read by the author), $12.95.

I Marry You Because . . .

Poetry and quotations on love and marriage. 192 pages. **Trade paperback,** $5.95.

PORTRAITS: A Book of Photographs

The first published collection of Peter McWilliams's photographs focuses on portraits of people. The book is a large format (9x12) and features more than 200 black & white and color photographs, exquisitely printed. 252 pages. **Hardcover, $34.95.**

Ain't Nobody's Business If You Do
The Absurdity of Consensual Crimes in a Free Society

The idea behind this book is simple: As an adult, you should be allowed to do with your person and property whatever you choose, as long as you don't physically harm the person or property of another. 818 pages. **Hardcover, $11.47. Paperback, $5.95.**

That Book About Drugs

The war on drugs is proving to be one of the most costly—and deadly—wars in U.S. history. We may not approve of drugs, but does it make sense *to put people in jail* for doing what *we* think is not a good idea? **Paperback, $5.95.**

What Jesus and the Bible <u>Really</u> Said About Drugs, Sex, Gays, Gambling, Prostitution, Alternative Healing, Assisted Suicide, and Other Consensual "Sins"

What the Bible actually says about these activities is, for the most part, not what we're told the Bible says about them. This book is surprising, entertaining, and informative. **Paperback, $5.95.**

To order any of these books,
please check your local bookstore, or call

1–800–LIFE–101

or write to

Prelude Press

8159 Santa Monica Boulevard
Los Angeles, California 90046

Please write or call for our free catalog!

ABOUT THE AUTHOR

CHRISTOPHER McMULLEN

PETER McWILLIAMS has been writing about his passions since 1967. In that year, he became passionate about what most seventeen-year-olds are passionate about—romance—and wrote *Come Love With Me & Be My Life*. This began a series of poetry books which have sold nearly four million copies.

Along with romance, of course, comes loss, so Peter became passionate about emotional survival. In 1971 he wrote *Surviving the Loss of a Love*, which was expanded in 1976 and again in 1991 (with co-authors Melba Colgrove, Ph.D., and Harold Bloomfield, M.D.) into *How to Survive the Loss of a Love*. It has sold more than two million copies.

He also became interested in meditation, and a book he wrote on meditation was a *New York Times* bestseller, knocking the impregnable *Joy of Sex* off the #1 spot. As one newspaper headline proclaimed, MEDITATION MORE POPULAR THAN SEX AT THE *NEW YORK TIMES*.

His passion for computers (or, more accurately, for what computers could do) led to *The Personal Computer Book*, which *TIME* proclaimed "a beacon of simplicity, sanity and humor," and the *Wall Street Journal* called "genuinely funny." (Now, really, how many people has the *Wall Street Journal* called "genuinely funny"?)

His passion for personal growth continues in the ongoing LIFE 101 SERIES. Thus far, the books in this series include *You Can't Afford the Luxury of a Negative Thought: A Book for People with Any Life-Threatening Illness—Including Life*; *LIFE 101: Everything We Wish We Had Learned About Life In School—But Didn't* (a *New York Times* bestseller in both hardcover and paperback); *DO IT! Let's Get Off Our Buts* (a #1 *New York Times* hardcover bestseller); *WEALTH 101: Wealth Is Much More Than Money*, and *LOVE 101: To Love Oneself Is the Beginning of a Lifelong Romance.*

His passion for visual beauty led him to publish, in 1992, his first book of photography, *PORTRAITS,* a twenty-two-year anthology of his photographic work.

Personal freedom, individual expression, and the right to live one's own life, as long as one does not harm the person or property of another, have long been his passions. He wrote about them in *Ain't Nobody's Business If You Do: The Absurdity of Consensual Crimes in a Free Society; That Book About Drugs;* and *What Jesus and the Bible Really Said About Drugs, Sex, Gays, Gambling, Prostitution, Alternative Healing, Assisted Suicide, and Other Consensual "Sins."*

In 1994, after successfully being treated for depression, he wrote with Harold H. Bloomfield, M.D., *How to Heal Depression.*

His fifteen-year sojourn through John-Roger's destructive cult, the Church of the Movement of Spiritual Inner Awareness (MSIA), is documented (with a surprising degree of humor) in *LIFE 102: What to Do When Your Guru Sues You.*

All of the above-mentioned books were self-published and are still in print.

Peter McWilliams has appeared on *The Oprah Winfrey Show, Larry King* (radio and television), *Donahue,* and *Sally Jessy Raphael.* He lives in Los Angeles.

Index

A

T

The difference between
the actual truth
and the illusion of truth
is what you are about to learn.

You will not finish learning it
until you are dead.

LORD LAURENCE OLIVIER